Praise for *What Every Christian Needs to Know About Passover*

"Rabbi Moffic draws from Jewish wisdom in a way accessible to all of us. His insights as a rabbi speak generously to a multi-faith world."
—**Eugene H. Peterson**, author of *The Message* and Professor Emeritus of Spiritual Theology, Regent College

"Rabbi Moffic's book is a treasure for people of all faiths. I've been celebrating Passover all my life, but I learned things in this book I'd never known. The book is a pleasure to read, filled with wisdom and inspiration."
—**Sara Davidson**, author of *The December Project* and *Loose Change*

"Rabbi Moffic creates a feast for the mind and heart as he sets the table for a rich Passover experience. Historical events, biblical texts, and stories from Jewish communities through the centuries make for an engaging read. His conversational style and personal anecdotes inspire readers to explore the richness of the Passover in their own homes, and he offers a seder script to help get started."
—**Lynn H. Cohick**, Professor of New Testament, Wheaton College

"When I finished reading Rabbi Evan Moffic's wonderful book, I was left with one insight: When we understand our differences, we discover our commonality. While presenting us with the amazing history and rich understanding of Exodus and Passover and explaining words, objects, and Jewish rituals, we become aware of experiences common to our faith and to all humankind—the hunger for freedom (freedom from and freedom to), hope that will never die, and the ongoing dreams of what life can be for Jews, Christians, and all people. Passover reveals that our homes are sacred—temples of the Divine. Breaking bread is holy communion. We discover a unity with one another and with our God. Your life and your faith will be richer and fuller thanks to this book and the marvelous wisdom of Rabbi Evan Moffic. However, I will make one suggestion. The title should be *What Every PERSON Needs To Know About Passover*."
—**Fr. John Cusick**, Catholic Archdiocese of Chicago

"Vividly written and full of history and insights. It is an experience rich in cultural definition that will heighten and enlighten your own faith walk."
—**Patsy Clairmont**, author of *Twirl: A Fresh Spin at Life*

"The spiritual roots of every Christian go back to Jesus, and the spiritual roots of Jesus go back to Judaism, and the spiritual roots of Judaism are sunk deep in the promise and practice of liberation. Rabbi Evan's *What Every Christian Needs to Know About Passover* is a wonderful way to water those roots."
—**Rabbi Rami Shapiro**, author of *Let Us Break Bread Together: A Passover Haggadah for Christians*

"Passover is a universal story of freedom whose message is needed now more than ever. Rabbi Moffic opens us to this Jewish holiday in a way that can speak to people of all faiths."
—**Lonnie Nasatir**, Anti-Defamation League

Further Praise for Rabbi Moffic

"People everywhere are seeking a better way to live. Many have a faith tradition we call home—but sometimes moving outside that tradition helps us see resources we never knew were there. Through his stories and insight, Rabbi Evan Moffic shines the light of Jewish wisdom in a way that helps all of us find our way."
—**Reverend Christine Chakoian**, Senior Pastor, First Presbyterian Church of Lake Forest

"Rabbi Moffic has given us a generous guide to unlocking the power of our words—to God, ourselves, and each other."
—**Jeff Goins**, author of *Wrecked: When a Broken World Slams into Your Comfortable Life*

"Rabbi Moffic is an engaging teacher who excels at communicating ancient truths for modern audiences. His insights into Hebrew scriptures and the Jewish heritage of the Christian faith will be a blessing to all who want to learn."
—**Pastor Steve Gillen**, Willow Creek Community Church

"Rabbi Moffic is a captivating speaker for people of all ages. He shows the richness of the Old Testament and Judaism and gives insights into Jesus' Jewish context and character. Christians and Jews can benefit from his knowledge and from his character."
—**Ken Davis**, humorist and best-selling author

"Evan Moffic unlocks the wisdom of Judaism in a way that can enrich us all."
—**Dr. Eboo Patel**, founder and President, Interfaith Youth Core

"Evan Moffic is a rabbi, but he's also an extraordinary scholar and a teacher of the highest order. He can speak to us all, whatever our faith or culture. And he does it with grace, humor, and erudition. Such a guy."
—**Jim Kenney**, International Interreligious Peace Council, Interreligious Engagement Project, Common Ground

"Rabbi Moffic is one of the best young Rabbis and scholars I have ever heard speak and teach about both Judaism and Christianity. His wit, his humor, and his deep knowledge about the Old Testament and early Christianity will give insight into Jesus' Jewish context, history, and character."
—**Newton Minow**, former chairman of the Federal Communications Commission (FCC), Vice-Chair Commission on Presidential Debates

WHAT
EVERY CHRISTIAN
NEEDS TO KNOW
ABOUT
PASSOVER

WHAT
IT MEANS
and WHY
IT MATTERS

RABBI EVAN MOFFIC

Abingdon Press
Nashville

WHAT EVERY CHRISTIAN
NEEDS TO KNOW ABOUT PASSOVER
WHAT IT MEANS AND WHY IT MATTERS

Copyright © 2014 by Evan Moffic

All rights reserved.

Library of Congress Cataloging-in-Publication Data

Moffic, Evan, 1978-

What every Christian needs to know about Passover : what it means and why it matters / Rabbi Evan Moffic. — 1st [edition].

    pages cm

    ISBN 978-1-4267-9156-7 (binding: soft back : alk. paper) 1. Passover—Christian observance. I. Title.

  BV199.P25M644 2015

  296.4'537—dc23

2014040641

Text illustrations: Paul Soupiset

Scripture quotations unless otherwise noted are taken from the Common English Bible. Copyright © 2011 by the Common English Bible. All rights reserved. Used by permission. www.CommonEnglishBible.com.

Scripture quotation marked (NIV) is taken from the Holy Bible, New International Version®, NIV®. Copyright © 1973, 1978, 1984, 2011 by Biblica, Inc.TM Used by permission of Zondervan. All rights reserved worldwide. www.zondervan.com. The "NIV" and "New International Version" are trademarks registered in the United States Patent and Trademark Office by Biblica, Inc.TM

Scripture quotation marked KJV is from The Authorized (King James) Version. Rights in the Authorized Version in the United Kingdom are vested in the Crown. Reproduced by permission of the Crown's patentee, Cambridge University Press.

For the Haggadah, the author used his own scriptural translations from the Hebrew for the Old Testament.

This project uses the SBL Hebrew font, which is available from the Society of Biblical Literature at www.sbl-site.org.

14 15 16 17 18 19 20 21 22 23—10 9 8 7 6 5 4 3 2 1

For my grandfather, Dr. Ervin Hansher.
You lived the Passover story.
You live on in the hearts of your children,
grandchildren, and great-grandchildren.

"We are dwarves who sit on the shoulders of giants."
—Rabbi Isaiah of Venice, 1250

CONTENTS

INTRODUCTION

WHY PASSOVER MATTERS TO CHRISTIANS

Four thousand years ago a momentous meal took place. Sitting around the table were Moses, his brother Aaron, sister Miriam, and the multitudes of Israelites preparing to leave Egypt. It was the first Passover meal. Nearly 1,400 years later, Jesus sat at a similar meal with his disciples. The story of Moses and his leadership of the journey from Egypt to the Promised Land was retold. When Jesus and his friends ate that Passover meal, they were a small band of Israelites living in the midst of the oppressive Roman Empire, and Passover's story of freedom and resistance to powerful political rulers resonated with poignancy and passion.

Jesus' Passover meal, of course, became one of the most famous Passover meals in history. It both drew on and re-created the events of the original Passover from Egypt, and it foreshadowed the world-changing events of Jesus' death. It has been immortalized in innumerable pieces of Western art, most famously Leonardo da Vinci's masterpiece *The Last Supper*, and is remembered and reenacted by Christian communities around the world every time they celebrate Holy Communion (otherwise known as Holy Eucharist, or the Lord's Supper).

So the Passover meal is one of the interesting places that Judaism and Christianity intersect—intersections that are, at once, rich, complicated, winsome, and sometimes fraught. Jews—even Jews who observe very few other religious rituals—celebrate a Passover seder each year, a meal that commemorates the events of the origi-

nal Exodus from Egypt.[1] Churchgoing Christians celebrate Jesus'
Passover seder when they take Communion, and many Christian
communities specifically recall Jesus' Last Supper on Holy Thursday,
the Thursday before Easter. Finally, in recent years, a growing number of Christians have been attending Passover seders at the homes
of Jewish friends or relatives, or celebrating their own seders in their
church communities. This book, written primarily for Christian
readers, does not just "explain" the nuts and bolts of traditional
Passover seders, though it does do that. It does not just review what
the Passover meal probably meant to Jesus and his friends, though
it does that too. More fundamentally, *this book explores the radical
claim that one meal—one momentous meal, the Passover seder—can
in fact change your life.*

This meal can draw you closer to God, and can help you find
God's liberation from the places of scarcity, of imprisonment, that
lurk in your life. You will ponder anew the places in your lives
where you feel trapped and inadequate. You will see where God's
outstretched arm can renew your life and faith.

To enter more deeply into the liberation of the Passover meal, we
will join the Israelites on their journey from slavery to freedom. We
will see the tools God gave them to rediscover that freedom in every
generation by asking questions, praying, celebrating, and retelling
the story. As we do so, we will shed light on the journey of our own
lives. We will ask ourselves where we might be enslaved. Are we
enslaved to our possessions, our work, our addictions, our desire to
please others? Are we stuck in an Egypt that will not let us free? As
we ask these questions, we will join the ancient Israelites. We will
bring their story to bear on our own. *Passover is God's invitation for*

---

1. The Hebrew word *seder* means "order." It also refers to the Passover
meal itself. Because of its frequent usage, I do not italicize throughout the book.
Other frequently used words transliterated from Hebrew include *haggadah* and
matzah. Less frequent Hebrew words translated into English are italicized.

each of us to become free. It has extended over thousands of years, and this book is the chance to make it your own.

It may seem strange for a Jewish rabbi to write a book on Passover for Christians. I lead a large congregation in suburban Chicago and have devoted my own spiritual life to observing Jewish holidays, praying Jewish prayers, and studying Jewish texts. What do I have to say to Christians? A lot, it turns out. Many Christians have a yearning, I have discovered, to get closer to God by discovering the Jewish roots of Jesus and Christianity. In speaking and teaching at churches, I have seen the way Jewish wisdom can bring Christians closer to their faith. I have seen the way it can deepen the experience of prayer, expand the meanings of biblical passages, and open our eyes wider to the role of God in our lives.

Exploring the Passover story helps us learn more about the context of Jesus' own religious and spiritual life, and it sheds light on Easter, the resurrection of Jesus, and the meaning of redemption. But the magnificent drama and depth of the Passover story also gives us a powerful framework to understand the journey of our own lives. I have had students tell me the story of Passover helped them gain freedom from a difficult past. Others have told me the Passover story confirmed for them that God always keeps his promises, just as God did for the Israelites. The Passover story can speak to us wherever we are on the journey of our lives. My goal in this book is to help you discover what message this sacred story holds for you.

WHAT YOU WILL EXPERIENCE

In chapter 1 we begin our journey into the liberating story of Passover. We will revisit the first Passover meal in Pharaoh's Egypt and see the faith and leadership of Moses that made it possible. Through the chapter are scattered practical insights into and interpretations of the Exodus story from three thousand years of Jewish history and tradition. Chapter 2 brings us into the world of ancient Israel and discusses the way Passover was celebrated when Jesus lived and taught in Jerusalem. We experience the pageantry and sense of holiness that pervaded Jerusalem during Passover and imagine the promise of freedom it represented.

Chapter 3 takes us to the fertile period of religious life after the destruction of Jerusalem in 70 CE. We learn how ancient Jews sustained their faith when all seemed lost. We discover the new understanding they gave to freedom and how they preserved the Passover message when others tried to destroy it.

Then we get ready to eat! Chapters 4 through 8 walk us through the preparation for and meaning of the Passover meal. If you've ever had a dinner party at your home, you know the time and effort it requires. You have to cook a meal, find a table setting, and maybe even think of interesting topics of conversation. Now add on a layer of spiritual preparation. Jews read different sacred texts during the month before Passover to prepare our hearts and souls to accept freedom. Passover is a time of rebirth, and the preparation for it can be as spiritually meaningful as the holiday itself. Jews traditionally start preparing for Passover thirty days before it begins. You will see the way this time of preparation resembles the forty-day period of Lent, which is also preparation for the rebirth of humanity through Jesus. In experiencing the way Jews prepare for Passover, you may discover an even deeper meaning in Lent and Easter.

Chapters 9 and 10 bring Passover into the twenty-first century. They explore the way the themes of Passover have shaped contemporary struggles for freedom. The groups who embraced the Passover story as part of their struggle range from American slaves to Jews living in the Soviet Union during the 1970s and 1980s. The Passover story even shaped America's Founding Fathers, who saw their journey from oppression in the Old World to freedom in the New World as a modern expression of the Exodus story.

For the final chapter, I have compiled a script for a Passover meal (the script is known in Hebrew as a *haggadah*, which literally means "the telling") designed specifically for Christians interested in exploring and experiencing this ancient Jewish ritual. It will reflect the traditional Jewish explanations so as to give participants the best sense of what Jesus experienced and provide brief summaries of the contemporary Christian interpretations that have emerged alongside the Jewish ones.

AN INVITATION

I passionately believe that religious and spiritual people can learn from traditions different from our own—perhaps especially from those traditions that are our next-door neighbor traditions, which is how I think of Judaism and Christianity. As a rabbi, I have found great inspiration in the description of love from Paul's Letter to the Corinthians. My own prayer life has been transformed by what I learned from pastors and Christian writers. Quite often, I learn more about my own faith when I encounter it with new questions and concerns prompted by those who do not share it.

I believe the same growth can happen for Christians interested in deepening their own faith. Passover in particular holds spiritual invitations that can speak powerfully to Christians. Passover was observed by Jesus. It is a holiday centered around family, food, and freedom. It is accessible and relevant to Christians of all denominations.

So consider this book as an invitation: an invitation to explore the Jewish roots of your faith. An invitation to experience ancient texts and teachings—which for centuries were accessible only to a tiny group of scholars—and see the profound wisdom they contain for living a discerning, justice-oriented, loving life of service to God and neighbor. No book like this has been published before because the walls were too high. But we live now in an age when Pope Francis can say "Inside every Christian is a Jew" and the President of the United States can host a Passover seder at his house.[2] This book brings you into the story that shaped the Jewish people. In entering into that story you will discover your own.

---

2. See *Huffington Post*, June 13, 2014, www.huffingtonpost.com/2014/06/13/pope-francis-christian-jew_n_5492835.html.

CHAPTER 1

FROM SLAVERY TO FREEDOM

The Biblical Exodus

Sometimes our most important journeys begin in tragic circumstances. It may be the death of a loved one. It may be the loss of a job. We can feel trapped by these circumstances, and they can start to define us. I recall a member of a synagogue I served in Louisiana who had lost her husband tragically. She was in her sixties and quite healthy. She had many friends and a successful career. When her husband died, however, her life became defined by this loss. She took all the paintings down from the walls of her house, and replaced them with pictures of him. She changed her stationery to identify herself by her husband's first and last name. She even kept his voice on her answering machine.

Now contrast my Louisiana friend's journey with that of another parishioner from Chicago. She also experienced the loss of her husband at a relatively early age. He was a force of nature, a highly successful businessman and community leader. She mourned deeply. Many of their friends had been through him, and thus she felt somewhat disconnected from the wider community after his death. Yet, after about a year, she began to change. She started volunteering at a hospital and a grief counseling center. She became involved in the synagogue, which had earlier been a peripheral part of her life. She began a new path defined by the future rather than the past.

All of us grieve differently, and I probably should not judge someone for her feelings of loss. But it seems clear that the second parishioner found a healthier and more satisfying path. She experienced monumental pain, but she did not let tragedy define her future.

What meaning do we make out of tragedy and loss? That is the question that my two parishioners' experiences of bereavement pose to me. And it is also one of the fundamental questions of Passover. The Israelites had experienced profound individual and social loss through decades of enslavement, and God miraculously freed them—and then commanded them to observe a holiday in which they were to make some sort of sense, some sort of meaning, from their loss. God didn't tell the Israelites to forget their suffering in Egypt, or to just "move on." Rather, God told them to remember forever that they were slaves in Egypt. The Passover celebration is the medium through which Jews, over the centuries, have remembered and made meaning from the trauma of slavery.

Like my two parishioners, the ancient Israelites' journey began in tragic circumstances. After having lived as welcome residents of Egypt for hundreds of years, they are enslaved by a pharaoh determined to destroy them. They experience four hundred years of bitter slavery. Yet, after God leads them to freedom, they do not define themselves as victims. They do not seek revenge on the Egyptians. Rather, they hold the first sacred Passover meal telling their story of God's redemption. They derive the moral requirement to never oppress the stranger because they had been strangers in the land of Egypt. In other words, they seek to experience the blessing of freedom and not the pain of victimhood.

They begin their new journey by gathering for the Passover meal, the

The ancient Israelites' journey began in tragic circumstances. They experienced four hundred years of bitter slavery. Yet, after God leads them to freedom, they do not define themselves as victims. Rather, they hold the first sacred Passover meal telling their story of God's redemption.

oldest religious ritual in Western history, in which they tell a story that redefines who they are.

How did the Israelites transform themselves? What role did God play in their journey? How did they use memory and ritual to reframe the experience of slavery? Let's look at their story.

How Did the Jewish People End Up in Egypt?

The Jewish people arrived in Egypt 430 years before the Exodus. They came with the support of the then pharaoh, whose kingdom had been saved through the foresight and prophecy of the Israelite Joseph. Joseph was the second youngest of the Jewish patriarch Jacob's twelve sons. After being sold into slavery by his brothers, who were jealous of his special talents and their father's overt favoring of him, Joseph had used his wits and abilities to arrive at a position of power in Egypt. He served as Pharaoh's prime minister, saving Egypt from a seven-year famine that destroyed much of the surrounding area.

For a while, Joseph's descendants prosper in Egypt. Then, according to the Book of Exodus, "a new king came to power in Egypt who didn't know Joseph" (Exodus 1:8). This formulation is the Bible's way of telling us that this pharaoh did not know of the great contributions that the Israelite Joseph made to Egypt. He did not know the history of the Jewish people in the land. He was like a type of person we all know: someone who looks at others and asks only "what have you done for me lately?" Soon the pharaoh becomes paranoid. Fearing the growth of a non-native, non-Egyptian population that could turn against Egypt in times of war and also looking for cheap labor, this pharaoh enslaves the Israelites, demanding they work in building Egyptian cities and monuments. Pharaoh sought to destroy Israelite culture and unity so that they would not pose a threat to native Egyptians.

Despite these efforts to annihilate them, the Israelites survive. According to later biblical commentary, their population actually grows, and they become more unified as a people. They continue to use Hebrew names and refuse to succumb to Pharaoh's destructive policy. Their enslavement continues for four hundred years, but they remain a distinct people. They do not let persecution and hatred change who they are.

Four hundred years after slavery begins, however, a new pharaoh determines to destroy the Israelites once and for all. He decides to throw every male child born to an Israelite into the Nile River, thus draining their strength and eliminating future generations. Despite their efforts at maintaining their inner and outer strength, the Israelites feel despondent. They reach a bottom, seeing their future wiped out before them. *In any journey, however, the bottom has one advantage. There is nowhere to go but up. And it is at their bottom that the Israelites cry out to God, and God hears their cry.* God answers their cry through the figure of Moses. Moses renews the Israelites' hope. He renews their faith. And he shows them that though they may have been enslaved, faith can set them free.

WHO IS MOSES?

In Jewish tradition Moses is the greatest prophet the Jewish people ever had. He is the lawgiver, teacher, and scribe of God. He challenges Pharaoh, leads the people through the desert, and guides them to the edge of the Promised Land. His life ends on a poignant note, as God permits him to see the Promised Land from afar but not to enter it. Moses' final resting place is unknown because, according to the Jewish sages, God did not want the people to turn Moses into a divine figure. He is simply the Jewish people's greatest prophet. His story is the story of the Exodus.

Moses' birth seems to suggest he was destined for great things. Unlike the other Israelites, he never experiences slavery. He is born during the time when Pharaoh is killing all Israelite males at birth. Immediately after his birth, however, Moses' mother and sister place him on a basket and send it floating down the Nile River. His sister Miriam watches the basket from reeds beside the river, and she sees the daughter of Pharaoh take the basket and find the Hebrew child. In the Bible, Pharaoh's daughter has no name, but later Jewish commentators call her *Batya*, which means "daughter of God." Her compassion and humanity lead her to adopt Moses as her own son. She also hires Moses' mother and sister as his nurse and nanny, unaware of who they really are. Moses is raised in Pharaoh's palace, a "prince of Egypt," presumably afforded all the luxuries and opportunities of Egyptian royalty.

Everything changes the day he first leaves the royal palace. His age at the time is unknown, but later interpreters suggest he was fifteen. He sees Egyptian taskmasters whipping Israelite slaves. Although the text does not tell us how and when he learned he was an Israelite, Moses somehow knows the slaves are his people, and he acts to defend them. He kills one of the Egyptian taskmasters. The next day he sees a fight between two of the Israelite slaves. One of them taunts him and says, "Are you planning to kill me like you killed the Egyptian?" (Exodus 2:14) Moses realizes that word of his crime has begun to spread, and he will be a wanted man in Egypt. He flees for Midian, which is a desert land of shepherds and nomads. His first stop is at a well. He encounters a group of hostile shepherds attacking a group of seven sisters. Moses defends them and drives the shepherds away. He returns with the daughters to their home and meets their father, Jethro, a local priest. Moses soon marries one of the sisters he saved named Zipporah.

Each of these stories is significant because it reveals the core of Moses' character. He could not bear seeing a helpless slave beaten by an Egyptian taskmaster. He could not stay silent as two Israelites fought one another. And he could not stand by as Midianite shepherds attacked a group of defenseless sisters. *Moses does not stand idly by as others suffer and bleed. He is present. He is present to suffering. He is present to injustice. And he is present to God.*

HOW GOD MET MOSES

We see this presence to God most clearly in the next formative incident in Moses' life. The Bible tells us that while Moses was out walking with his flock, he hears God's voice speaking from a bush that burns but is not consumed (Exodus 3:1-12). Moses had to be present to hear that voice. In fact, the Jewish sages write that this bush had been burning without being consumed for years. Most people, however, did not notice it. They simply walked by. Moses noticed the burning bush and wondered why it was not consumed. When he turned around and paid attention to it, God spoke to him. His attunement to divine power made him worthy of leadership. Others had their opportunities. But Moses responded. The Hebrew word he used in answering God's voice highlights his readiness to act. Moses says "*Hineni*, I'm here" (Exodus 3:4).

What does God tell Moses? According to the text, God has now "clearly seen" Israel's oppression at the hands of the Egyptians (Exodus 3:7). God has chosen Moses to lead the Israelites to freedom. God reminds Moses that he is an Israelite and that his ancestors Abraham, Isaac, and Jacob were God's faithful servants. God tells Moses his time to act and lead has arrived.

WHO IS GOD?

When Moses turned, he had a profound, dramatic, and in some ways quite intimate encounter with God—and the Bible's description of the encounter between God and Moses also reveals a core part of how Jews understand God. In an enigmatic verse, God says to Moses that he can tell the people that "*Ehyeh asher Ehyeh*" sent him (Exodus 3:14). This particular divine name—*Ehyeh asher Ehyeh* (אֶהְיֶה אֲשֶׁר אֶהְיֶה)—does not occur anywhere else in the Bible. It does not even seem like a proper name. In Hebrew the phase means "I will be what I will be." Some English Bibles translate it as "I am Who I am." Or "I am What I am." The Hebrew is written, however, in the future tense: "I will be what I will be," or "I will become what I will become."

Why does this difference matter? How might it shape our own understanding of God? I believe it teaches us how the Bible wishes us to understand God. God is not static. God is dynamic. God is not defined by the past. God is experienced in the future. *What I will be, God is telling Moses, depends on what you and the people do. God is a becoming, and not just a being.* In fact, the Hebrew language does not have any word like the English "is." In Judaism, as reflected in the Hebrew language, identity is never static, and never unalterable. Like God, we are dynamic, evolving, ever changing, and ever growing. We may have had a miserable upbringing. We may have done things in the past we are not proud of. But those things do not define us. We define ourselves in the future. And the future shapes how we are remembered.

My favorite example of this truth is physicist Alfred Nobel. He invented dynamite and made a tremendous fortune. When he died, however, he left that fortune to create a prize for a person or group that best promotes peace. And we remember his name through that prize—the Nobel Peace Prize. God is telling Moses—just as he is telling us—your journey is not over. Your people will not be slaves forever. With God's help, they will become free. God cares about who we will become, not just who we have been. God sees our potential and invites us into the future.

God's revelation to Moses also gives Moses confidence. He hears God's instruction, and finds a strength he did not know he had. After

God appears to him at the burning bush, Moses is no different physically. Yet, he is different spiritually. After having hesitated and feeling unsure about the work God has for him, Moses accepts God's call, and he returns to the Egyptian royal palace. He comes before Pharaoh and tells him "This is what the LORD, Israel's God, says: 'Let my people go'" (Exodus 5:1). Pharaoh's first response seems to convey genuine shock. This shepherd, whom he had probably known as a boy growing up in the royal palace, is demanding he free a huge population of slaves. He does so in the name of the Israelite God, while Pharaoh sees himself as a god. To put it in contemporary nonreligious terms, it would be as if a farmer from a poor and distant country like Bangladesh demands that the president of the United States do something at the behest of the president of Bangladesh. Pharaoh understandably challenges Moses' request. "Who is this LORD whom I'm supposed to obey by letting Israel go? I don't know this LORD, and I certainly won't let Israel go," he replies (Exodus 5:2).

Moses and Aaron repeat their demand. Pharaoh refuses, and chides them for distracting the Israelites from their labor. He demands they leave and then tells the chief Egyptian taskmaster to toughen the Israelite labor requirements. In particular, he tells the taskmaster to take away the straw the Israelites used for making bricks, but still require they make the same number of bricks each day. They would have to go out and find their own straw, making their labor longer and more strenuous. Pharaoh seems to be trying to turn the Israelites against Moses by punishing them for Moses' impetuous behavior.

The ploy works. They blame the messenger. They beg Pharaoh to relent, and he tells them they are lazy. They swear at Moses, telling him God will judge him harshly for his actions. These criticisms are the first of many Moses receives as he leads the Israelites out of Egypt. He pleads to God for guidance, and God tells him to keep doing what he is doing. God is telling Moses to be patient because

God has larger plans. God is setting up the confrontation with Pharaoh that will lead to freedom. God then tells Moses to return to Pharaoh and demand once again that Pharaoh free the Israelites.

An emboldened Pharaoh responds by daring Moses and Aaron to prove the power of their God and perform a miracle. Aaron takes his staff and turns it into a snake. Pharaoh's magicians do the same thing, but their snake is eaten by Aaron's. Still, Pharaoh remains unmoved. He rejects Moses' demands to free the Israelites. God then inflicts the first of ten plagues upon the Egyptians. He turns the Nile River into blood. The Nile is the life source of Egypt. It waters its crops and serves as Egypt's source of influence. Turning it to blood undermines Egypt's strength. Yet, Pharaoh dismisses it as an amateur trick his magicians could do. His heart remains unmoved.

God's next plague is to cover the land of Egypt with frogs. Pharaoh begs Moses to stop it, promising to free the Israelites when the frogs are gone. Moses does so, but then Pharaoh reneges on his promise. In describing these events, the Bible emphasizes that God knew Pharaoh would renege. Indeed, God hardened Pharaoh's heart, ensuring he would resist letting the Israelites go free and the plagues would continue.

I have always been troubled by this idea that God hardened Pharaoh's heart. Does that mean God takes away Pharaoh's free will? Does that mean God desired the plagues to continue so as to inflict massive destruction on Egypt? It seems that way. What kind of God would do that?

These questions have stumped Jewish interpreters for centuries. The most accepted answer is that God hardening Pharaoh's heart allowed Pharaoh to continue to follow his heart's true desires. He did not want to give in. But the harshness of the plagues and the growing opposition of his courtiers tempted him to simply accede to Moses' requests. *God therefore preserved Pharaoh's free will—his desire to continue to enslave the Israelites—by hardening his heart and making him incapable of turning back from confrontation with Moses.*

Other theologians suggest Pharaoh lost his free will during the first six plagues. Free will is not absolute. Pharaoh had six chances to repent. When he did not do so, his character had become so corrupted that he lost the ability to change course. It was as if he became caught in a spider web and could not get out of it. God did not need to harden Pharaoh's heart because it was already a solid rock. By saying God hardened Pharaoh's heart, the Bible is simply emphasizing how wicked Pharaoh was.[1]

I don't find any of these answers completely convincing. The best response I can give to the text is to suggest it teaches the difference between Moses and Pharaoh. Moses attunes himself to God's word. He is present to God at the burning bush and his life is transformed. Pharaoh, on the other hand, has a hardened heart. He cannot listen. He is not present. He is indifferent. Both Moses and Pharaoh hear the same God. But they respond differently. By highlighting these differences, the Bible is trying to teach us how to open ourselves to God's presence. We are to be like Moses—present, engaged, listening, letting God guide us in the unfolding of our journey, rather than closing our hearts as Pharaoh did.

Both Moses and Pharaoh hear the same God, but they respond differently. The Bible teaches us how we are to be like Moses— present, engaged, listening, letting God guide us in the unfolding of our journey, rather than closing our hearts as Pharaoh did.

By opening ourselves up to God on our journey, we also open ourselves up to one another. This teaching helps us understand the ninth plague, the enclosing of Egypt in total darkness. The darkness was so thick that "people couldn't see each other" (10:23). This verse cannot mean only physical darkness. If that was case, people could just light lamps. Rather,

---

1. This point of view is outlined in psychologist Erich Fromm's classic text *Escape from Freedom* (New York: Holt, 1994).

it was a darkness that infected the heart and soul. Physically, the Egyptians were able to see, but psychologically and spiritually, they were not able to feel or care for one another. This is what the Torah means when it says the "people couldn't see each other." They were blind to one another's needs. Each person acted for and saw only himself or herself.

Perhaps the Bible is suggesting that a total absence of faith in our lives can make us blind to one another's needs. Pharaoh and the Egyptians were utterly indifferent to God's voice and commandments. Thus, they became utterly indifferent to one another.

THE MOST GRUESOME PLAGUE

The final plague haunts us to this day. It is the death of all the firstborn sons in Egypt. It happens on the night when Israelites put blood from a lamb on the doors of their homes so that the angel of death would "pass over" them on its journey through Egypt. This plague works. It leads Pharaoh to relent and let the Israelites leave. Still, it leaves us with many questions.

Why hurt thousands of Egyptian families on account of the intransigence of Pharaoh? God seems to be inflicting collective punishment on a gruesome scale. What did the firstborn sons of Egypt have to do with enslaving the Israelites? Is God condoning the death of innocent Egyptians? Does Passover celebrate those deaths?

The Jewish sages struggled with these questions. Through the ritual of Passover, however, they offered a compelling answer. During the Passover meal, when the plagues are recounted, we let a drop of wine fall from our wineglasses for each plague. For the final plague, we let two drops spill. The drops represent the tears of the Egyptians. They suffered because of their despotic leader, and we respond with empathy. When others suffer, we do not rejoice. We do not take pleasure in others' pain. We open our hearts and share their tears.

A TRANSFORMATIVE MOMENT

The tenth plague devastates Pharaoh, and he agrees to let the Israelites leave. Pharaoh, however, soon changes his mind, as God said he would, and leads an army in pursuit of the Israelites. The army catches up with them, and by the time the Israelites reach the shores of the Red Sea, they are terrified. The plagues and hasty march will end in their death and destruction.

Then their journey reaches a transformative moment. They witness a miracle. As Pharaoh's army closes in, God splits open the sea. The Israelites cross, and the sea closes in on Pharaoh's troops. As they reach the banks of the other side of the sea, the Israelites begin to sing a song of freedom. They dance. They celebrate.

This scene of redemption is engraved on our minds. Why is it there? Surely God could have simply whisked the Israelites across. Why the drama of opening and closing the waters of the sea? I believe it teaches us that sometimes, extraordinary inexplicable things happen on our journey. And when these things happen, we can only stand in awe and sing God's praise. We can all have these experiences, and they do not have to be as dramatic as the splitting open of the sea.

I remember sitting one day with my three-year-old daughter. She had a book in her hands and was turning the pages and telling the story. This was her regular habit. She could not yet read the words, but she could tell the story based on the pictures. I had one ear listening to her voice and the other, I am sorry to say, thinking about the coming week's sermon. Suddenly I stopped thinking about the sermon. I turned my head toward her. Something was different. I looked down at the book. I realized she was not telling the story in her own words. *She was reading the words on the page.* I couldn't believe it. Time stood still for a second. Then I looked at her, laughed, smiled, and started to sing. I didn't sing any particular song. It was just words of joy and happiness, and we both started dancing around the room. That was a transformative moment. *It was a time on my journey when the waters parted and I glimpsed God working in the world.* By splitting open the sea in front of the entire Israelite people, God is telling us we can all have those moments. We only have to be present and attune our souls to recognize them.

My daughter's learning to read was not the end of her journey. It was just the beginning. In fact, the next night I asked her to read a different book for me. She replied by telling me she did not know how to read. She wanted me to read to her. This continued for several nights. Knowing how to read was exciting but also a little scary. The same was true for the Israelites. The crossing of the sea was magnificent, but now they faced forty years of wandering in the wilderness. They began to have doubts. They started to backslide. They cursed Moses and pleaded for the comfort and security of Egypt. How did they make it through this part of their journey? What kept their faith? We will discover the answers they gave—and they truths they teach us—in the next chapter.

CHAPTER 2

RITUALS
OF FREEDOM

*The Celebration of Passover
During the Lifetime of Jesus*

When we have a sacred experience in our lives, do we move on and forget about it? Let's say we go on a mission trip and build homes. It changes us. Do we then come home and say "That was a great week. Let's do it again next year?" Or let's say we go on a pilgrimage to Israel. We feel deeply connected to the land and to the biblical events that happened there. Do we return and say, "That was fun. Where are we going on our next trip?" No. A true spiritual transformation changes us in ways we never imagined. We strive to keep the memory alive. We work to keep the flames kindled. One of the ways we do so is through ritual. Let's take the example of a pilgrimage to Israel: if we go and it changes us, perhaps we decide to go back every year or every other year. Or perhaps we decide to contribute to an Israeli charity every month. We need to sustain the experience through ritual. This is what the Israelites did with Passover. Passover was not just a one-time event. It became an annual reliving of the Exodus journey that lasts to this day. Let us explore how they did it.

THE TEMPLE AND THE PROMISED LAND

After crossing the Red Sea the Israelites wandered in the desert for forty years—and then they finally crossed over into the Promised Land. Once there they built a Temple in Jerusalem. It was built on

Mount Moriah, where, in the Book of Genesis, Abraham had followed God's command to prepare his son Isaac as a sacrifice. This Temple became the center of Jewish religious life. The priests managed the operations of the Temple, and with the assistance of the monarchy, they centralized all animal sacrifice in Jerusalem. While some local temples persisted, the Jerusalem Temple was the focus of religious life and a destination for pilgrimages for several major holidays. Among these holidays was Passover—the annual reliving of the Israelites' Exodus from Egypt. Every year, while the Temple stood, people traveled from all over to celebrate Passover at the Temple— it is Passover that Mary, Joseph, and the young Jesus are celebrating in Jerusalem in the second chapter of the Gospel of Luke. Indeed, many thousands of people came to the Temple for Passover.

Every year, while the Temple stood, people traveled from all over to celebrate Passover at the Temple— it is Passover that Mary, Joseph, and the young Jesus are celebrating in Jerusalem in the second chapter of the Gospel of Luke. Indeed, many thousands of people came to the Temple for Passover. And when they got there, they found a massive, grand celebration.

And when they got there, they found a massive, grand celebration. The Talmud (a sacred compendium of Jewish law and lore compiled between the third and sixth centuries CE) mentions the hundreds of ovens set up in Jerusalem to roast the Passover lambs. Another source, the scholar Philo of Alexandria—who lived in the first decades of the Common Era, when the Temple still stood— described the scene in Jerusalem: "Multitudes of people from a multitude of cities flow in an endless stream to the Holy Temple for each festival . . . from the east and west, from the north and south."[1]

1. Philo, *On Laws*, 1:96.

Why did Passover generate so many visitors? Perhaps because it was the ancient Jewish version of July 4th. It celebrated national liberation and freedom. One might think the small city of Jerusalem could not handle so many pilgrims. The Talmud suggests that God delivered a miracle that made it possible. We read in the rabbinic work *Ethics of the Fathers*, that "while standing in the courtyard of the Holy Temple, all the people would be pressed close together . . . but yet when it came time to bow prostrate, all would have ample room."[2] Jerusalem somehow expanded and made space for all who came. This miracle, according to the Jewish sages, was one of the ten miracles that occurred during the time the Jerusalem Temple stood.

We catch a glimpse of this history in the Gospels as well. Near the end of his life, Jesus enters with the flock of pilgrims going into Jerusalem the week before Passover (Matthew 21–22). It was not uncommon for pilgrims to arrive the week before Passover so they could prepare themselves spiritually for the holiday. They would undergo purification rituals like immersing the *mikva* (purification bath). In Judaism water is a means for purification, as it became in Christianity as well. Non-Jews from across the Roman Empire also came to Jerusalem during Passover. It was an exciting time, and an entire space in the Temple was reserved for Gentile pilgrims.

After undergoing these rituals of purification, families would bring an unblemished lamb to the Temple. A priest would slaughter it, and the family would serve the lamb as they retold the Exodus story at the Passover meal that evening.

Even after the Temple was destroyed in 70 CE and Jews were forbidden from living in Jerusalem, the memory of this paschal celebration persisted. Every Passover seder meal, as we will discuss in the next chapter, ends with the saying, "Next year in Jerusalem." This saying is not only about the next year chronologically. It also hints at the religious vision of the end of days, a time when the Jewish

---

2. *Pirke Avot* ("Sayings of the Fathers"), 5:7.

people will be restored to the land of Israel, and Jerusalem will once again house a functioning Temple. Redemption begins with freedom and a return of the Jewish people, led by God, to the Promised Land. Saying "Next year in Jerusalem" expresses hope for that redemption, and faith that it will eventually come about.

This ritual sacrifice of the paschal lamb was one of two ways Jews during the time of the Temple—the time of Jesus—celebrated and remembered the Exodus. The second ritual, *Chag HaMatzot*, the Festival of Matzah, focused on the eating of unleavened bread. The unleavened bread hearkens back to the moment when the Israelites finally gained their freedom. After the death of the Egyptian firstborn sons, Pharaoh agreed to let the Israelites go. They gathered their belongings and rushed out of Egypt. They did not have time to eat, or bake bread that rose. Matzah—unleavened bread (Exodus 12:33-39)—was the only thing they had time to make and eat, since they could not wait in one place for long.

In biblical times the Festival of Matzah was a weeklong remembrance of this hasty journey. It typically began after the Passover meal, and Jews would eat matzah at home, in the marketplace, and in the synagogue. When the Temple no longer stood, Jews began to practice Passover rituals at home, including the ritual meal (modeled on the Temple sacrifice of lamb) and the weeklong eating of matzah. What had been two distinct but related Passover commemorations during the era of the Temple melded, after the Temple's destruction, into one rich household celebration of the holiday of Passover.

I'm always amazed at the creativity and insightfulness of this ritual remembering of Passover. Our ancestors had to figure how to make the moment of redemption last. It could easily be forgotten, as we know happens throughout history. They were dedicated to keeping the memory and the values it embodied alive, and they used food and community in order to do so. Memory was ritualized.

The brilliance of their method hit me recently when I returned from a group trip to Israel. The group consisted of fifty men, all of whom are either lay or professional leaders in the Jewish community. The goal of the trip was to learn about Israel and show our support for its people. We also, however, explored some of our shared concerns as men. We talked about fatherhood, work pressure, being good husbands, and finding meaning beyond professional success.

I found the trip transformative. Yet, we only go to Israel as a group once a year. How do we maintain the bonds and reinforce the values we embraced on the trip? We gather for regular meals and discussion. We eat Israeli food to remind us of the trip and talk about places we visited. We study sacred texts connected to our visit and to issues of fatherhood, family, and personal meaning. We keep the memory and meaning of the trip alive through ritualized meals and study. It has worked so far.

THE CENTRAL ROLE OF SYMBOLS ON OUR JOURNEY

The men on my Israel trip did not choose to eat Israeli food because it is particularly good. We did so because it reminded us of the experience we shared. The ancient Israelites did the same thing. Matzah is not a particularly tasty food. But it captures several of the meanings and moral imperatives of the Exodus journey.

First, in reminding us of the limited time the Israelites had to escape, the matzah symbolizes the fragility of freedom. The Israelites had to rush out of Egypt. They could not stop for moment. *When we taste the matzah, we recognize that our lives and the blessings we enjoy are indeed fragile. Tasting the matzah can help us cultivate gratitude for those fragile blessings.*

This lesson of gratitude is further developed when explore other meanings of the matzah. Consider a teaching of a great sixteenth-century rabbi from Prague known as the Maharal. He highlights the biblical description of matzah as *lechem oni*, which means "bread of affliction."[3] The matzah traditionally symbolizes the affliction, the torment of slavery in Egypt. The Hebrew word *oni*, however, can also mean "poverty." Matzah is the bread of poverty, but not poverty in the sense of suffering. It is poverty in the sense of simplicity. It is poverty in the sense of depending on nothing but God. Matzah depends on nothing but water and flour. It lacks any processing or sweetening. It has no nonessential ingredients. It lacks flavoring or seasoning. It is pure. As the Israelites left Egypt, their faith was pure. They depended on nothing but God, and God brought them redemption. At some points in our journey we will be like the ancient Israelites. We will depend on nothing but God. The matzah reminds us of this truth.

Matzah depends on nothing but water and flour. It has no nonessential ingredients. As the Israelites left Egypt, they depended on nothing but God, and God brought them redemption. The very simplicity of the matzah teaches us about the condition of true freedom. We lack freedom when we are dependent on material things.

The very simplicity of the matzah teaches us about the meaning of true freedom. We lack freedom when we are dependent on material things. When we must have something in order to enjoy something else—when we must have wine with dinner, for example, or one particular brand of clothing—we are not truly free. The fewer and more basic our needs, the freer we are. Matzah symbolizes that freedom. It represents the process in which we journey from slavery to freedom. We remove all the bonds and dependencies that enslave us to other people or things. We find freedom in the symbol of matzah: Freedom is simplicity.

Indeed, this emphasis on simplicity runs throughout the Bible's stories of Exodus, wilderness, and the Promised Land. Consider the place where God gives the Israelites the Torah and the Ten

3. Maharal of Prague, *Magen Avraham*, 471:5.

Commandments. It is on a small mountain in the barren desert. Freedom does not come from a glorious place on high. It comes from modesty and simplicity. God could have revealed those commandments anywhere. He chose a small mountain in the wilderness. The wilderness consists of the sand, the sky, and nothing else. It is a place where God can have a direct encounter with the people. The people are not distracted by sights and sounds. They can focus their mind and heart on God.

Each of us can encounter God in simple places. A minister I know first experienced God's call to service while praying in a little suburban park by his house. We do not need to be in a grand or fancy cathedral. We can be in a soup kitchen: this is where I was at age thirteen when I first felt a call to become a rabbi, as I watched with awe and admiration as the rabbi of my synagogue served and pastored to the people there. We can be in a nursing home. We can be in a wood hut in Africa or a street corner in America. *Experiencing God depends not so much on what is happening outside of our bodies, but on what is going on inside of our souls.* As we taste the matzah, we are meant to open ourselves to the possibility of change, of faith, of transformation. We open our mouths and try to let God into our hearts.

THE NEXT STEP ON THE JOURNEY: COUNTING THE OMER

Matzah was a central symbol of Passover during the Exodus and remained so when the Temple stood. Yet, Jewish life changed dramatically during that period. Jews went from a wandering group of nomads in the desert to a settled people in the land of Israel. Thus, during the lifetime of Jesus—when the Temple stood—Jews commemorated the Exodus with the paschal celebration and the festival of matzah. But over the years, this two-pronged holiday of

Passover took on a third aspect, one not directly connected with the original Exodus. Faithful Jews also began to see Passover as a time to celebrate a critical moment in the agricultural calendar and the harvest. This connection made sense because the land's produce was seen as dependent on God's favor. Thus, on the second day of Passover, farmers would cut down the first sheaf of the barley harvest. A measure of this grain was called an *omer*. Between the second day of Passover and the beginning of the holiday of Shavuot (later known in Christianity as the Pentecost), farmers would harvest barley. They would count the harvest each day. On the final and fiftieth day, Pentecost, farmers from across Israel would bring the first wheat offering to the Temple in Jerusalem.

This practice ended, however, after the destruction of the Temple in 70 CE. Few Jews remained in Israel to farm the land. Thus, the Jewish sages altered the observance of this fifty-day period. Rather than mark the harvest, the sages turned to the Bible and made it into a time to celebrate the connection between the Exodus from Egypt and the giving of the Torah at Mount Sinai. According to the Bible, forty-nine days elapsed between the time the Israelites left Egypt and the time they arrived at Mount Sinai. On the fiftieth day, God revealed the Torah to Moses, and the people accepted it as their law. Today we count the seven weeks between Passover and Pentecost and use them as a time to cleanse and prepare ourselves spiritually. Certain sacred texts are read. We mark each day by saying a blessing and stating which of the fifty days it is. Why do we say a blessing? It makes us aware of the possibilities of each day. It offers the potential for inner growth. We can also follow a practice of Jewish mystical tradition and focus each day on a certain quality of character or teaching. In my own practice, I choose a different value to focus on each day and a unique biblical passage to consider.

Making each day count is a powerful idea. But what does it have to do with Passover, the Festival of Freedom? *The essence of freedom is having control over our time.* It's ours to count, not someone else's to manage. Sustaining freedom also requires action. The great British Jewish philosopher Isaiah Berlin, whose family had fled Europe during the Nazi period, distinguished between two different kinds of freedom. Negative freedoms are "freedoms from." These include freedom from slavery, from persecution of religious expression, or from unjust imprisonment. But these freedoms are insufficient for human flourishing. Instead, they provide the context for positive freedoms. Positive freedom rests on the ability to choose our own path in life. It emerges in our ability to make decisions, to pursue opportunities, to use our gifts. Negative freedoms provide a context for a life of faith and purpose. Positive freedoms are the way we realize them.[4]

The Exodus from Egypt symbolizes the imperative of negative freedoms. Counting the Omer begins our realization of the positive ones. Neither has meaning without the other. America's founders understood this philosophical truth. They captured it in an early American patriotic slogan, "eternal vigilance is the price of liberty." Counting the Omer is a vigilant defense of freedom. It heightens our appreciation for what happens at its end, the giving of the Torah at Mount Sinai. Now that we are free from external oppression, we prepare ourselves for this positive opportunity by blessing and counting the days. We remember that the Exodus has not ended the journey. The most important part is yet to come.

FREEDOM NEEDS RESPONSIBILITY

There is a Jewish saying about the reason the Israelites had to spend forty years wandering in the wilderness. It says, "It took four days to take the Jews out of Egypt. It took forty years to take Egypt

---

4. See Isaiah Berlin, *Four Essays on Liberty* (Oxford: Oxford University Press, 1990).

out of the Jews." The saying is a cute way of highlighting the challenge of freedom.

True freedom is discovered not in the absence of responsibility. It is found in the development of ourselves, and that takes time and growth.

There is a Jewish saying about the reason the Israelites had to spend forty years wandering in the wilderness. It took four days to take the Jews out of Egypt. It took forty years to take Egypt out of the Jews. True freedom is discovered not in the absence of responsibility. It is found in the development of ourselves, and that takes time and growth.

One of my favorite Jewish teachings uses clever wordplay to teach this idea. In describing the tablets on which the Ten Commandments were carved, the Bible says, "The tablets were the work of God; the writing was the writing of God, engraved on the tablets" (Exodus 32:16 NIV). The Hebrew word for "engraved" is *charut*. Here's the clever wordplay: In the Talmud the rabbis write, "Read not *'charut*, engraved' but *'cherut*, freedom,'* for the only person who is truly free is one who occupies himself with learning and growth."[5] Through a slight change in the vowels of the word, the sages transform its meaning. Through study and spiritual growth, we engrave freedom in our hearts. We learn freedom by internalizing responsibility. *When the word of God becomes part of our minds and hearts, we become truly free.*

If this idea seems too abstract, consider a parent and a child. When a young child crosses a street, a parent needs to hold his or her hand and make sure the child crosses in safety. Over time, parents teach the child to look both ways, to follow the traffic signs, and to be careful and walk quickly to the other side. Once the child has internalized those rules—once it becomes part of his or her nor-

---

5. *Pirke Avot* ("Sayings of the Fathers"), 6:2.

mal behavior—the child does not need to hold the parent's hand. Through internalizing the rules—through having faith in them—the child has become able to do more on his or her own. He or she has gained a measure of freedom.

Freedom and responsibility also go hand in hand in our spiritual lives. For me the *greatest spiritual freedom is the capacity to grow and change.* We are not stuck where we are. We can grow closer to God throughout our lives. Following this path demands responsibility. For me the best indicator of this responsibility is prayer. When I am praying regularly—in the morning and the evening—I know I am nurturing my inner life. It does not always happen. Sometimes the day seems to fill with appointments and obligations. But if I go too long without regular prayer, my mind and soul wither. I seem to lack the freedom to grow.

The ancient Israelites also turned to prayer as a means of spiritual growth. This turn began in earnest after the destruction of the Jerusalem Temple by the Romans in 70 CE. This event shattered the world they knew, and prayer became the means by which they remembered the past and found hope for the future. The holiday of Passover became the story by which they assured themselves of God's redemption. They invested it with new meanings and ritual. Let us see how they did it.

CHAPTER 3

AROUND THE TABLE

Why Passover Is a Holiday
Celebrated Primarily at Home

What happens when everything changes? Perhaps we have to move suddenly. Perhaps we lose a job or a parent dies. Do we remain the same person? Yes, but we also change. Change is an inevitable part of our life's journey, and we all deal with it differently. If we are people of faith, we listen for God's voice. We try to discern what God is asking us to do.

Seeking God's direction is what both Jews and Christians did in the tumultuous period of first-century Judea. The Romans had grown more aggressive. The Jerusalem Temple was on the brink of destruction. Both groups looked for God's message in the midst of these crises. In certain ways, what one community heard from God differed from what the other community heard—but they also each looked to the Passover story as a guide for what God desired for them.

For Jews, Passover became a home-based celebration. We discovered that the most important lessons are taught in our most intimate place: the home. The central act of that celebration was prayer. The home was seen as a miniature temple in which our words and deeds and even the food we ate served God. The lessons of freedom and God's deliverance were not only proclaimed at temple. They were lived at home. When crisis struck, the Jewish people turned inward for strength. We found it in abundance.

HOW THE HOME BECAME A SANCTUARY

First, a little background. For centuries, as we learned in chapter 2, the Temple, and sacrificial worship at the Temple had been at the heart of how the people of Israel worshiped and connected with God. In 70 CE, that Temple was destroyed by the Roman army. Jews had to find new ways of keeping their faith alive and communicating with God. Instead of bringing sacrifices of animals and grains as a way to interact with God, they developed a rich prayer book based on the prayers of the Psalms, which they had always prayed. Instead of celebrating the central holidays of the faith at the Temple, they found new ways to celebrate, often at home. Because rabbis took on new importance after the Temple was destroyed—it was rabbis who collected taxes, enforced the ritual laws, and negotiated with Rome—post-Temple Judaism became known as "rabbinic Judaism." The form of Judaism they established also shaped the life of Jesus and became the backdrop against which Christianity developed.

With the Temple destroyed, the Jewish people could no longer observe the feast of the Paschal lamb. The rabbis needed to figure out a new way to observe Passover. A core premise of their faith was that the Torah is eternal. Therefore, they could not conclude that God's word no longer applied. God still intended for the Israelites to observe the Passover. They just needed to discern the way God expected them to do so without the Temple or sacrificial lamb.

The way the rabbis reshaped Passover became the paradigm by which they transformed other Jewish holidays, and the principles guiding them have shaped Jewish life ever since.
The form of Judaism they established also shaped the life of Jesus and became the backdrop against which Christianity developed.

The way the rabbis reshaped Passover became the paradigm by which they transformed other Jewish holidays, and the principles guiding them have shaped Jewish life ever since. Their principles were often unstated, but still unmistakable. First, they transferred the holiness that dwelled in the Temple into the family home. The home became a *mikdash me-at*, a miniature temple. Second, the table where food was served was reimagined as a miniature altar. And third, the priesthood became the prerogative not just of a small hereditary group, but of every Jewish person. In short, the rabbis introduced a form of democracy into religious life. The justification for this change was founded Exodus 19:6, which describes the people of Israel as "a kingdom of priests . . . and a holy nation."

THE HOME IS THE TEMPLE

The rabbis' theology flowed from recognition that home is where we learn the basics of life. It is where we learn our most important lessons. Indeed, Jesus frequently teaches in homes because in Judaism they are the center of religious life.

Thus, when the Passover lamb could no longer be offered at Temple, the celebration of the Exodus moved to the home. The home became a festival place, filled with food and family. The Jewish philosopher Philo writes about this beautifully. "On this day [Passover]," he writes, "every dwelling-house is invested with the outward semblance and dignity of a temple."[1]

Where do our most formative events happen? Where do we learn the basics of life? At home. That's where first-century Jews learned their most important lessons. Indeed, Jesus frequently teaches in homes because in Judaism they are the center of religious life.

---

1. Quoted in Baruch M. Bokser, *The Origins of the Seder* (New York: Jewish Theological Seminary Press, 2002) 9.

This sanctifying of the home also drew from the practices of the surrounding Hellenistic culture throughout the second and third centuries of the Common Era. This was the culture of Palestine and much of the ancient Near East. The upper classes within this culture would frequently participate in a festive meal known as a symposium. Plato's book *Symposium* provides an example of what happened during such a meal. Intellectual exchange and debate were interspersed with food and toasts. Participants often reclined.

The Passover meal shares many of these characteristics. Participants seek to experience the feeling of freedom by reclining. The discussion centers on the meaning of the Exodus from Egypt. Eating and drinking are interspersed with the discussion. Even the name for the ritual dessert—*afikomon*—is of Greek origin.

The Greek symposium, however, lacked something sacred. It lacked the presence of God. The Passover meal has never been just an intellectual feast and drinking party. It is a reenactment of a divinely ordained journey from slavery to freedom. In retelling this story as a group around a table, the rabbis created what scholar Jacob Neusner calls "table fellowship." They invested the human practice of eating with sacred ritual and discussion.[2]

We can appreciate the wisdom of this focus when we consider our culture. How do we treat most meals? Are they occasions for holiness? Rarely. They are too frequently occasions for rapid digestion and eyes glued to the TV or iPads. In my own home, with two young children, most meals are occasions for at least one spilled drink. My wife and I celebrate if we get through a meal unscathed by liquid, stray food, or a sibling fight.

The Jewish sages recognized, however, the pragmatic and sacred role of a communal meal. The Jewish people had been riven by conflict with Rome. They had also experienced great internal con-

---

2. See Jacob Neusner, *From Politics to Piety: The Emergence of Pharisaic Judaism* (New York: KTAV, 1979).

flict between different groups vying for power. They needed a way to keep the fledging community together. They needed a way to focus energies toward building a more pious community rather than outward inward toward building a military-based community that would surely be crushed by Rome. Sacred meals—centered around prayer and discussion—were the best vehicles for doing so. They build personal ties and generate communal holiness. They bring different people together over something we all share: a need for nourishment and friendship. They also create memories. Memory is essential to faith. We remember what happened to our ancestors. We derive meaning and direction from those memories.

I know this personally. I have so many memories of Passover seders. I remember hearing my grandfather sing Passover songs. I remember some particularly long meals where I put my head on the table and almost fell asleep. I remember taking my newborn daughter to her first Passover meal three weeks after she was born. She was perched in a little chair between my wife and me, and I was praying some of joy of the songs seeped into her heart. *If you have only been to a Passover seder at a church or synagogue, I urge you try it at home. The memories created there last like no other.*

GOD IS EVERYWHERE

By refocusing Jewish practice on the home, the rabbis also addressed a big theological issue. Ancient Jews believed God's presence dwelled in the Jerusalem Temple. It was God's home on earth. When the Temple was destroyed, was God destroyed as well? Some said yes. Tens of thousands of Jews assimilated into Roman culture following the Temple's destruction. But a larger group said no. The Temple was not primarily about God. It was about the people. They needed a place to feel God's presence. For a thousand years the Temple was that place. But its destruction did not mean God's destruction. God could be found and experienced anywhere. God's presence could be felt at home. God's presence could be felt in the market. Most importantly, God's presence was felt in the midst of community.

The Temple was not primarily about God. It was about the people. They needed a place to feel God's presence. For a thousand years the Temple was that place. But its destruction did not mean God's destruction. God could be found and experienced anywhere.

This idea allowed Judaism to survive after the destruction of the Temple. Sacred acts could be performed anywhere. One of the names the rabbis frequently used for God illustrates this truth. In various teachings, the rabbis refer to God as *HaMakom*, meaning "The Place." The original reason the rabbis give for using this name for God is to teach that God's presence is not limited to the physical world. It extends across the universe and every dimension of time and space. Over time and through specific usage, however, this particular name for God came to symbolize the idea that God's presence was accessible anywhere in which a Jewish community lived and followed God's law.

If God is not limited by space, what brings God into focus? How do we access God's presence? In rabbinic Judaism, the answer became community. God dwells among the people. A biblical verse hinted at the idea the rabbis developed. The verse says, "They should make me a sanctuary so I can be present among them" (Exodus 25:8). The rabbis read this verse carefully. God does not say "Make me a sanctuary so I can be present in *it*." God is present "among them." God's presence does not depend on the physical space. It rests among the people. A physical space does not possess holiness on its own. It only receives holiness from the people who gather there. We see this idea reflected in the life and message of Jesus. Even when the Temple stood, God's presence felt inaccessible to many Jews. The

Temple felt remote and was managed by a small group of priests who often reserved privileges for themselves. Thus Jesus, like many other Jews, railed against its corruption. It symbolized a God who dwells only above, and not a God who dwells in our hearts.

Rabbinic Judaism embraced the idea that when people gather together, they make space for God. The Passover meal in a family home exemplifies this practice. Thus, as a Christian exploring the story of Passover and the experience of the Passover meal, you are invited to experience the unique sacredness of trying a Passover meal at home. Most Christians I have spoken with have been to a seder at either a church or synagogue. Experiencing it in a home, however, makes the encounter with God even more intimate. People are more at ease with one another. We open ourselves up more. *Both Jews and Christians believed God created the world as a home for humanity. We model God by inviting others in our own home. The Passover story feels more personal and relevant in our home.* We may be using our own china. We are sitting in our own chairs. We are running back and forth to our own kitchen. And if we invite others, we invite them into a deeper side of ourselves. We are not simply chatting at a restaurant or a church function. We are sitting around a table like family.

In my own spiritual journey, a formative moment happened around a Passover table. It was at the home of one of my college professors. I had always been in awe of this professor. He was tall, brilliant, and spoke fast. You would ask him a question, and he would cite ten books that addressed it. I admired his intellectual rigor. Then during my junior year, he invited me to his home for Passover seder. I was a bit nervous. He could be intimidating in the classroom. I became even more nervous when I realized one of the other guests was Chelsea Clinton, who was a year behind me at Stanford. When I walked into his home, however, a different side of him came into view. His kids ran through the halls laughing. He greeted me as he walked down the stairs with a basket full of laundry. Chelsea and a few other students were helping set the table.

The seder itself was an intellectual feast. He taught us several interpretations that found their way into this book. But it was also filled with laughter, family stories, and even a few spills.

I had always been moved by this professor's mind. Now I was taken by his heart. I experienced a similar shift in my relationship with God. Study had always been my spiritual passion. Part of what was appealing to me about Jewish tradition was its embrace of the life of the mind. But as my journey progressed, I became more impressed by the words of the heart. I began to love prayer. I began to see the personal transformation and comfort in pouring my heart out to God. In the wake of the destruction of the Temple, the Jewish people saw that truth as well. They poured their heart out to God in the home, and thereby kept the relationship with God alive and vibrant. Passover is one of the ways we celebrate that relationship today.

CHAPTER 4

CLEANSE YOUR SPIRIT AND CLEANSE YOUR KITCHEN

How to Prepare for a Passover Seder

We have now investigated the biblical account of the first Exodus and delved into the history of how Passover was celebrated during the life of Jesus. Now it is time to turn to how Passover is celebrated in Jewish homes today. The first thing to know about a Passover seder is that it takes a lot of preparation.

I know this firsthand. When my wife, Ari, and I hosted our first seder, we prepared for years. Literally. We began in the months before our wedding. We were filling out a gift registry at Bloomingdale's. Ari signed us up for a beautiful set of Passover china. "We'll need it when we host our first seder," she said. "We'll have our parents, my brothers, your sister, maybe some members of your synagogue."

I swallowed. I would have preferred going to my parents' home for seder. Yet, I agreed. I secretly believed no one would get the Passover set for us because it was too expensive. It turned out we had generous friends. The Passover set was one of the first items purchased off the registry.

A few years later, we had the chance to use it. The china came in handy, but it was the least of our concerns. First, we had to clear the house of bread. We will learn why later in the chapter. Then we had to e-mail our guests to know their food allergies. Next, we had to make sure we had enough books for everyone and enough toys and distractions for the kids. We had to make sure we had a prize for the child who found the *afikomon* (as well as consolation prizes for everyone else!). We also constantly feared we would not live up to the seeming perfection of our parents' Passover meals. We both remembered them as flawless and fun. They set a high standard we didn't think we could meet.

I began to wonder whether all this preparation was detracting from the spiritual meaning of the holiday. Did worrying too much about silverware make it harder to move closer to God? Not if we approach the preparation with the right attitude. Anything serious requires preparation. We gain more satisfaction when we put more effort into something. Think about Easter. The preparation time of Lent—which involves rigorous behavior and sacrifice—makes Easter all the more powerful. The same is true with Passover. Preparing for Passover is about much more than purchasing the proper food. It is a time for thorough physical and spiritual cleansing of our homes and hearts. It involves acts of cleaning, studying, and giving charity. Now we will explore how to make this preparation meaningful.

A TIME TO PREPARE

According to the Jewish sages, preparation for a holiday begins thirty days before the day itself—and roughly thirty days before Passover is the Jewish holiday of Purim.[1] Purim is a time of celebration and farce, costuming and drinking. Many refer to it as the Jewish Halloween or Mardi Gras. When it concludes, serious preparation for Passover begins. The rabbis do not give a definite reason why preparation for a holiday begins thirty days before the holiday. In the case of Passover, however, the thirty days of preparation hearkens back to the biblical origins of the holidays. According to the sages, the Israelites needed to find the appropriate lamb to

---

1. The primary book of Jewish law was compiled in the sixteenth century and is known as the *Shulchan Aruch*. This teaching is found in Section *Orach Chayim*, chapter 429, verse 1.

bring to Jerusalem to offer as a sacrifice. This lamb had to be free of blemishes. Selecting the right lamb and preparing it for travel could take thirty days. In addition, Passover is also a holiday observed at home. Preparation has to begin early so families can be thorough and seek advice and answers from a rabbi as to what they need in their home. In addition, since the process of removing leaven from the home begins in the week prior to Passover, people customarily start to watch what they purchase and use in the home about thirty days before Passover.

Jewish tradition forbids the eating of any type of leavened bread during the seven days of Passover in order that we remember the haste with which the Israelites had to leave Egypt. They had no time to let their bread leaven, or rise. To ensure no accidental consumption of leaven, it has become customary to totally clear our homes of it. Eliminating leaven from the home requires a thorough inspection of the house. Even small morsels are forbidden. The rabbis outline the process by which we search for them. To understand this process, we first need to know what we are looking for. It is not simply bread. It is anything that contains leaven. Even the smallest bit of leaven and anything with the potential for unintentionally creating leaven has to be found and discarded.

If this practice seems extreme, consider the precautions some children and adults have to take today to avoid peanuts or gluten. Someone with celiac disease cannot eat anything with bread. Even the smell of peanuts can trigger reactions in certain people. We take the prohibition on leaven just as seriously.

Aside from helping us remember the Exodus from Egypt, thoroughly eliminating leaven from our midst embodies psychological wisdom. If we do not see any bread or bread products during Passover, we will not be tempted to eat them. Our minds will feel more at rest with what we must do. I realized this psychological wisdom when my wife and I dealt with our daughter's celiac disease. She had a much easier time avoiding bread products when we simply eliminated them from our house. Doing so is not easy in the short run. But it saves enormous willpower and avoids greater conflicts in the long run.

What needs to be eliminated? The Bible says *Lo yera'eh lecha chametz, velo year'eh lecha se'or bechol gevulecha*—"neither *chametz* (grain that ferments) nor *se'or* (sourdough—highly fermented dough that is used to make another dough ferment) shall be visible to you in all your boundaries" (Deuteronomy 16:4, my translation). The primary difference between the two is that *chametz* is an edible product and can be eaten outside of Passover and *se'or* cannot. Cereal, for example, is *chametz*. The yeast (leaven) that ferments beer is *se'or*. Some types of alcohol are permitted on Passover. The yeast used in the fermentation cannot have been grown on bread. The rabbis also created one other category called "garbage." It is nonedible leaven that cannot ferment other dough. An example of "garbage" is deodorant. It may very well contain some grain products. But it cannot be used to ferment other grains. Thus, we are not required to eliminate it from our homes for Passover.

THE SEARCH FOR LEAVEN

Now that we know what we are looking for, how do we go about finding it? The rabbis developed a thorough and logical process. Not all Jews follow this process. Yet, many make every effort to eliminate most *chametz* from their homes.

1. Clean all places where *chametz* may have been eaten or might be found. It is customary to look under the cushions on the sofa, in the pockets of pants, under desks, light switches and even on closet floors. After a room has been thoroughly searched and emptied of *chametz*, it is declared *pesadik* (fit for use on

Passover), and no *chametz* is to be consumed in that room until after Passover.

2. Empty and scrub the refrigerator to remove all traces of *chametz*. Wash the inside of the freezer as well.

3. Scrubbing the oven, stove tops, and rack and turning their heat on high for an hour so as to burn any remaining *chametz*. This process is called "kashering." We also "kasher" a microwave by boiling water inside of it for at least twenty minutes.

4. Bringing out a new set of dishes and silverware reserved for use during Passover. The dishes and utensils normally used are washed and put away. Some families even have a separate dishwasher for the Passover china, though that is not essential.

5. Clean the kitchen and dining room tables of *chametz* by pouring boiling water over them and then scrubbing with soap and water. They are then covered until Passover begins.

6. Clean countertops and chairs and other appliances with boiling water and soap. Vacuum and scrub floors. Wash the windows. Clean out cars and other overlooked places.

7. The night before Passover begins, conduct the final check of the house. Known as the *bedikat chametz*, it is traditionally done with a candle and feather to make sure dark and hidden places are searched. After the *bedikat chametz*, a home is ready for Passover.

This inspection lends itself to a thorough house cleaning as well. In fact, scholars trace the custom of spring cleaning back to the Jewish practice of clearing the home of leaven. In the Northern hemisphere, Passover typically falls near the beginning of spring. Cleaning the home for Passover became the perfect means for cleaning the home for spring.

Explanations abound for the thoroughness and significance of the Passover spring cleaning. The only reason given in the Bible is that we need to remove *chametz* from our homes and eat matzah in order to remember the Exodus from Egypt. Throughout Jewish history, however, the sages have given many meaningful reasons for this process of purging one's home of leavened products. One is that ridding our homes of *chametz* reminds us to watch our egos. *Chametz* is dough that expands and becomes "puffed up." Gratitude—one of the core values of the Passover—is impossible when our egos get puffed up. Thus, we refrain from eating any puffed up leaven.

A thorough inspection for *chametz* can also spark greater self-inspection. *Chametz* symbolizes the spiritually corrupting part of our human nature known as *yetzer harah*, the evil inclination. Judaism does not have an idea of original sin. Rather, each person is driven by two primary impulses: the *yetzer hatov*, the good inclination, and the *yetzer harah*, the evil inclination. Prayer and religious acts (known in Hebrew as *mitzvot*) cultivate the power of the *yetzer hatov*. Disobeying God's commandments nourishes the *yetzer harah*. When we avoid *chametz*, we weaken the power of the evil inclination. *When we watch what we eat, we are more likely to watch what we do.*

Cleaning our homes of *chametz* also helps us enter a new frame of mind. In several ancient Near Eastern cultures, spring marked the beginning of the New Year. In ancient Israel, Passover was considered the beginning of the new year, though this dating practice changed around the beginning of the Common Era. A thorough spring cleaning made possible a new beginning, and a feeling that the year ahead could be different than the past one. This interpretation is highlighted in the practice of taking breadcrumbs from our homes and throwing them into a body of water before Passover. We are throwing away our past so we can build a new future. In that future we need more than just bread. We need God.

By not eating bread for eight days, we remind ourselves we can survive without bread but not without God.

Indeed, our Jewish ancestors were mindful of the spiritual dimension of life. By not eating bread for eight days, we remind ourselves that we depend not on bread, but on God. We do not reject bread all the time. It is part of God's creation. *Yet, we remind ourselves that we can survive without bread but not without God.*

GIVING CHARITY

Preparing for Passover can create a burden for families with little means. Purchasing matzah and other foods that can be eaten on Passover requires extra money. So does a different set of dishes, which is needed to avoid any contact with bread. People also generally wear their finest clothes for the Passover. And cooking and serving a Passover meal with guests can be a financial burden.

In biblical days, a family that could not afford to bring a lamb to the Temple in Jerusalem would share a lamb with another family. The principle behind this practice was that finance could not be a barrier to religious observance. To make observance possible, it became customary in the Middle Ages for the community to ensure that all of its members had the ability purchase the foods required for Passover and participate in a Passover meal. The community's leaders would create a welfare fund to provide families with *maot chitim*, which literally means "wheat money." This money was used by families to purchase foods that could be eaten during Passover. This welfare fund was distinct from the general welfare fund that operated all year. According to the rabbis, Passover observance was so important that a separate fund needed to be created to ensure everyone had the ability to do so. Those who gave to the general welfare fund still had to give a special gift for *maot chitim*. No other holiday has this practice.

This unique obligation derives from Passover's underlying theme of freedom. No person is truly free if he or she does not have the means to eat. Furthermore, the opening lines of the Haggadah (the booklet read during Passover, which we will discuss in the next chapter) are "Let all who are hungry come and eat!" The obligation of charity ensures this verse rings true.

The creation of a fund is often accompanied by active participation in the distribution of food. Many families prepare food and deliver it in person to needy or elderly families. This personal participation reinforces the idea of community. Passover celebrates the liberation of the entire Jewish people from Egypt. Freedom was not limited to a select few. It was a shared experience. The eleventh-century biblical commentator Rashi points to a verse from the Bible to argue that experiencing the Exodus molded the disparate group of people into one strong community. The verse comes from Exodus 19:2, where the Israelites are at the foot of Mount Sinai. They have escaped Egypt and are preparing to receive the Torah. Then we learn, "Israel camped there in front of the mountain." The text uses the singular verb form for the word camped. Usually, the subject *Israel* is followed by a plural verb form. Here it is singular. Rashi says at that moment, the community was "like one person with one heart."[2]

Personal participation helps restore this idea of community. Passover can bridge the cultural divides between the rich and poor, the young and the old. This sense of unity Passover brings is especially evident in Israel, where every grocery store and restaurant abides by the Passover restrictions. Israelis experience a palpable sense of unity in eating the same general foods. From the array of ethnic restaurant we have in America, we know how powerful a cultural symbol food is. Passover celebration reinforces a cultural unity for Jews, and we work to ensure that everyone can feel part of it. It can also reinforce the shared principles of Judaism and Christianity, as we share a sacred meal together.

---

2. Rashi on Exodus 19:2.

IS PREPARING FOR PASSOVER LIKE EXPERIENCING LENT?

Like the time of Passover preparation, the Christian period of Lent encourages self-examination and an attention to life's details. For forty days, typically between Ash Wednesday and Maundy Thursday, Christians engage in introspection and refrain from eating rich and heavy foods. Some engage in several fast days. And some churches remove accessories like flowers from the sanctuary. Lent is preparation for the celebration of remembering the crucifixion on Good Friday and the resurrection of Jesus on Easter Sunday. At first glance, preparing for Passover and engaging in the discipline of Lent seem to have little in common. Preparing for Passover does not have to take place over forty days, nor is it given a distinct name like Lent that denotes its religious significance. It *is preparation for Passover*, and not the observing of it. Yet, this superficial contrast hides a deeper resonance between Lent and Passover preparation. Unpacking this resonance requires us to understand a fundamental truth about Judaism. Judaism is not a religion in the conventional sense. That is, it is not a set of doctrine and practices meant to define the relationship between an individual and God. These are part of Judaism, for sure. But Jewish living is much more encompassing.

The best definition of Judaism was given by the late twentieth-century philosopher Mordecai Kaplan. He defined Judaism as a "civilization," with cultural norms, a language, and habits. Judaism is not primarily a doctrine in which one believes, but a people with which one identifies. In Judaism, Kaplan said, belonging precedes believing. Identification comes before ideology. A person identifies with the Jewish people, and then the practices and beliefs may follow.[3]

---

3. See Mordecai Kaplan, *Judaism as a Civilization: Toward a Reconstruction of American Jewish Life* (Philadelphia: Jewish Publication Society, 2010; original 1932).

In Christianity, by contrast, believing usually precedes belonging. It is not primarily an ethnic or cultural inheritance. A person is baptized or saved, and thus becomes a Christian. Christianity is a religion as scholars typically define them. Judaism, however, is a culture, a people, and a religion. It does not fall neatly into any of these traditional categories. As a result, certain behaviors or practices that might not be construed as religious actually serve as an expression of a person's Jewish identification. Put differently, many Jews do not draw a sharp distinction between religious and nonreligious acts. What we eat matters as much as how we pray. What we say and how we spend money matter as much, if not more, than what we may believe. This truth helps us understand the parallel between Passover preparation and Lent. For Jews observing Passover, the preparation is just as important as the meal itself. Clearing *chametz* from the home is as significant as eating matzah. It is a time for spiritual cleansing. It requires discipline and self-awareness.

Both Lent and Passover preparation also draw their inspiration from the Exodus story. Lent traditionally lasts for forty days. This number is derived from the time Jesus spent fasting in the desert after his baptism by John the Baptist. This forty-day period was highly significant because just after it ended, Jesus began teaching in public and gathering disciples. Indeed, according to the Gospels, after these forty days, "news about him spread throughout the whole countryside. He taught in their synagogues and was praised by everyone" (Luke 4: 14-15). These forty days were preparation for proclaiming the message of salvation. This number and purpose parallel the Israelite experience during the Exodus. They lived in the wilderness for forty years. These forty years were preparation for experiencing redemption in the Promised Land. The number forty also reminds us of the four hundred years of slavery the Bible tells us the Israelites experienced in Egypt.

A further connection is found in the notion of rebirth. Both Passover and Lent take place in the spring, the time when nature renews itself. Lent culminates in Easter, celebrating the resurrection of Jesus and, effectively, the rebirth of humanity. The notion of humanity's rebirth is even marked in the Western calendar, where the birth of Jesus becomes the beginning of a new era starting with the year one. Birth does not happen automatically. Just as a baby gestates in a mother's womb for nine months, so the birth of the world requires preparation. Lent is that period of preparation. For Jews, Passover celebrates the rebirth of the Jewish people. During the four hundred years of slavery, the Israelites grew from a clan of seventy to a nation of over a million. When they left Egypt, they gained a new life in a new land with a new set of laws. The Passover meal is a time when we participate in that

Both Passover and Lent take place in the spring, the time when nature renews itself. Lent culminates in Easter, celebrating the resurrection of Jesus and, effectively, the rebirth of humanity. The notion of humanity's rebirth is even marked in the Western calendar, where the birth of Jesus becomes the beginning of a new era starting with the year one. Birth does not happen automatically. Just as a baby gestates in a mother's womb for nine months, so the birth of the world requires preparation. Lent is that period of preparation. For Jews, Passover celebrates the rebirth of the Jewish people.

rebirth. We experience what the ancient Israelites experienced. Thus, preparing for Passover is like getting ready to be reborn.

A dietary parallel also exists in the practice that some Christians have of observing a raucous "Shrove Tuesday" or "Mardi Gras." Shrove Tuesday is the day before Ash Wednesday, the day before the penitential Lenten season begins. Some Christian communities eat pancakes that evening as part of the process of ridding one's home of sugar and butter for the following six weeks of Lent. In other places, people eat rich foods as part of Mardi Gras celebrations. The underlying purpose is to prepare oneself for the period of self-denial of Lent. This Shrove Tuesday practice holds echoes of Christianity's origins. Before Easter was celebrated, the early Christians observed Passover, albeit with a different understanding than traditional Jews. Jesus became the Paschal Lamb who was sacrificed for humanity's sins. Yet, the early Christians likely cleared their homes of leaven in preparation for the Passover meal, just as Jews did. While the way in which this preparation takes place has changed, its underlying purpose has not. We cleanse our bodies so we can clear our souls and experience redemption.

PRACTICAL PREPARATION

We have prepared our homes and spirits. Now we have to make some resource allocation and personnel decisions. The most critical resource we will use during the Passover meal is a book known as the Haggadah. The Hebrew word *haggadah* literally means "the story." Today it is the book containing the liturgy followed during the Passover meal, and it includes the retelling of the story of the Exodus from Egypt. You will find a complete Haggadah in chapter 10 of this book.

The first complete manuscript of the Haggadah dates to the tenth century. It is part of a collection of Jewish prayers and holiday rituals compiled by Rabbi Saadia HaGaon, the greatest Jewish sage of the ninth century. This manuscript also constitutes the first complete Jewish prayer book. The first Haggadahs produced as works in their own right were completed in the fourteenth century. Among the most famous of this group is a text known as the Sarajevo Haggadah. Composed in Barcelona in the middle of the fourteenth century, it has an extraordinary history spanning wars and thefts, black-market sales and close calls with destruction. Its history became the subject of a best-selling book. It was sold to a museum in Sarajevo in

1894 (hence the name Sarajevo Haggadah) and was hidden from the Nazis during the Second World War. Some of its pages are stained with wine, indicating its frequent usage over the centuries. It opens with thirty-four pages of remarkable biblical scenes from creation through the death of Moses. Like the Sarajevo Haggadah, many Haggadahs contain rich illustrations. Their purpose was not to convey the story to those who could not read, since the entire story was recited orally. Rather, they illuminated the story and enhanced the experience for participants.[4]

Today thousands of different Haggadahs are available. They are both similar and vastly different. They are similar in that they contain mostly the same blessings. The four questions, which we will discuss later, and blessings for the four cups of wine are included in all Haggadahs. They differ in interpretations offered, additional prayers given, art adorning the pages, and themes described in the text.

The type of Haggadah you choose rests on several factors. The first is time. A traditional seder can last through the night. Each ritual can spark conversation and debate, and verses can be sung and repeated. Most seders, however, last between two and three hours. This includes about an hour for the first part of the seder; an hour to enjoy the meal; and about forty-five minutes for the concluding portion. Some seders intended for families with young children can be done in half an hour. Haggadahs intended for use in such a seder would include less commentary and an abbreviated retelling of the Exodus story.

The second factor governing the choice of Haggadah is theme. Different groups have adapted the story of Passover to reflect an issue or social concern important to them. During the 1960s, for example, several individuals created Haggadahs for "freedom sed-

---

4. For an overview of the history of Haggadahs, see Yosef Hayim Yerushalmi, *Haggadah and History* (Philadelphia: Jewish Publication Society, 1995).

ers" that compared the struggle of African Americans to the experience of the ancient Israelites. In the 1970s, a group of women wrote the first "Feminist Haggadah" that sought to recover and highlight the role of women in the Exodus story. In the 1930s and 1940s, Jews in Israel issued "Zionist Haggadahs" comparing the journey of Jews from exile in Europe to freedom in Israel to the ancient Exodus from Egypt. If a social or political issue has caught the attention of a significant group of people, it may well have generated a themed seder. Some participants may find this approach injects too much politics into a religious holiday. Yet, most of the themed Haggadahs contain the traditional rituals and prayers.

A third related factor is ideology. The Jewish community is divided amongst three major denominations. They are Reform, Conservative, and Orthodox. Reform is the largest, primarily because of its strength in America. Orthodoxy tends to dominate in other places. Orthodoxy believes that God communicated the entire Old Testament to Moses at Mount Sinai exactly as it is. Jews are obligated to observe all of the commandments. Conservative and Reform both say God inspired human beings to write the Old Testament, and other divinely inspired people wrote commentaries on and derived laws from it. The Conservative denomination teaches that any changes in laws and practices should happen slowly and only with the approval of rabbis who are experts in Jewish law. Reform views change more positively, arguing that the only way Judaism survives is when it is flexible enough to adapt to the surrounding culture while maintaining its unique message and way of life. These differences are broad characterizations, and some Reform Jews might have some beliefs and practices considered more Orthodox and vice versa. Yet, the broader differences do manifest themselves in the Haggadahs produced by leaders in each denomination.

Reform Haggadahs often avoid using gendered language for the name of God. Instead of referring to God as "He," the Reform Haggadah will substitute "The Holy One" or "The Eternal One."

Reform Haggadahs also contain convey a more social and political message, using the Israelites' Exodus story as a template for social movements throughout history. Some add rituals to honor the women heroes of the Exodus story. One Reform Haggadah even includes all the blessings in masculine and feminine Hebrew form.

Conservative Haggadahs tend to be traditional in the Hebrew text of the prayers and description of ritual. Yet, they will often use poetic translations and add English commentary more commonly found in Reform Haggadahs. Orthodox Haggadahs use the traditional Hebrew and often have a literal English translation. Rarely does an Orthodox Haggadah have modern commentaries or songs.

Other groups produce Haggadahs as well. The small denomination known as Reconstructionist Judaism produced a Haggadah entitled *A Night of Questions*.[5] It includes much of the traditional blessings, but emphasizes discussion and offers provocative historical questions about why we celebrate the Exodus even if the story may not be historically accurate. Some Jewish academic institutes have issued massive Haggadahs that tell personal stories from Passover participants from around the world and include many illustrations. Several Haggadahs incorporating stories and essays and special prayers related to Israel are also available.

The world's most popular Haggadah was actually produced by Maxwell House Coffee! In the 1920s, no coffee company made a product that could be used by Jews observing the Passover dietary laws. Thus, most drank tea during Passover. Maxwell House saw an opportunity and in 1923, as part of a promotional pitch, they compiled a Haggadah and gave it away to any family who purchased its new Passover-friendly can of coffee. The Haggadah became widely

---

5. Joy Levitt, ed., *A Night of Questions* (Philadelphia: Reconstructionist, 1999).

used in the United States and was recently reissued and has now been printed more than fifty million times.

There are a small number of Haggadahs produced specifically for Christians. One is by a past leader of the Jews for Jesus movement. Another was written several years ago by an excellent Christian scholar of Judaism. They focus primarily on offering a Christian interpretation of the traditional Jewish seder. They include many of the commentaries we will touch on in the subsequent chapter. I do not recommend using these Haggadahs as the primary guide for your Passover meal because they do not offer an authentic taste of what Jesus experienced. Although we will never know all the details definitively, Jesus likely experienced a traditional Passover seder guided by the blessings and rituals Jews have practiced for three thousand years. The stories and interpretations he heard are ones still taught at Jewish Passover seders today. They are ones we unpack here. In this book you are invited to experience the real thing.

CHAPTER 5

THE SEDER PLATE

*How Ritual Objects Connect Us
to One Another and to God*

In my parents' living room is an old piano. It's not in the best shape, and neither my mom nor dad plays piano. Still, it occupies the most prominent place in the living room. Why? My great-grandfather was a piano maker. He immigrated to the United States when he was sixteen and didn't speak a word of English. He went to school, started a piano shop, and ended up running three piano stores across Milwaukee. The piano in my parents' home is among the last he made. For them it symbolizes his presence. It captures his legacy for our family. It is deeply symbolic, carrying meaning far beyond its use as an instrument.

The Passover seder plate is the same way. Most Jewish families have a special Passover seder plate. They may keep it on a special shelf in the china cupboard. They use it only once a year, yet it is hugely important—far more important, perhaps, than any other plate in the house. For the Jewish people the Passover seder plate symbolizes our history. It captures the legacy of God's redemption of our ancestors, a group of slaves. It holds the central ritual foods used during the Passover meal. The seder plate is to Passover dinner what the chalice and paten are to the celebration of Communion, and the special foods on the seder plate are in some ways like the bread and the wine that the chalice and paten hold.

The seder plate can also speak to each of our personal stories. A few years ago I had Passover seder at the home of some parishioners. Before we began the meal, the patriarch of the family—a retired doctor in his seventies—told a story about the plate at the head table. He and his wife, Barbara, had lived in Switzerland in the early 1960s while he was in medical school. Barbara gave birth to their first child during exam week. They felt helpless. They had no family anywhere nearby. An elderly couple in their building volunteered to help watch the baby for two weeks while Harold finished exams. When exams were over, Harold and Barbara asked the older couple how they could repay them. The couple went into their cabinet, pulled out a seder plate, handed it to them, and said, "You can repay us by celebrating Passover and using this plate." They use that seder plate to this day.

MATZAH

The central symbols of the Passover seder are contained on the seder plate. The first of these is unleavened bread, known as matzah. Matzah is the symbol most associated with Passover, yet the primary commandment is simply to avoid eating leavened bread. The obligation to eat matzah only applies to the first night of Passover. Still, most Jews eat lots of matzah during the eight days of Passover, using it as a replacement for sandwich bread and snacking on it in place of typical crackers.

The central symbols of the Passover seder are contained on the seder plate. The first of these is unleavened bread, known as matzah. Matzah is the symbol most associated with Passover, yet the primary commandment is simply to avoid eating leavened bread. And the obligation to eat matzah only applies to the first night of Passover.

On the seder plate we find three pieces of matzah. On the Sabbath and all the other Jewish holidays, we typically bless two loaves of bread. This practice hearkens back to the ritual of the ancient Temple in Jerusalem, when holidays were accompanied by a double sacrifice. The Temple practice was derived from the manna God delivered to the Israelites in the wilderness. On the Sabbath and the festivals, God gave a double portion of manna, thus leading to double sacrifice in Temple times. In rabbinic Judaism, the loaves of bread replaced the sacrificial offerings, and thus it became the custom to have double loaves to accompany each holiday. On Passover, however, the third piece of matzah on the seder plate represents the special obligation of this holiday.

As we noted in chapter 2, matzah is the simplest of foods, containing just flour and water. Yet, Jews today distinguish between different kinds of matzah based on the way they are made. This distinction became relevant in the beginning of twentieth century with the emergence of machine-made matzah. Until then matzah had been made by hand. Some rabbis argued, however, for more use of machine-made matzah because the automated process made it less likely that the flour and water would sit for any significant period of time (eighteen minutes or more, according to Jewish tradition) and thereby ferment and become unusable. So long as the machine was kept clean and operating under the proper supervision, they argued, we should embrace its use.

Other rabbis, however, opposed vociferously the use of machine-made matzah. Their arguments reflect concern with an issue that all people of faith confront. How do we balance action and intention? Is the intent with which we do an act more important than the act itself? Is it necessary to have the right intention in doing an action if the result is the same without it? For the rabbis who opposed machine-made matzah, intent was critical. The Talmud argues that a commandment from God has to be done with the intent to fulfill a divine commandment. A machine has no intent when it is baking matzah. It is simply doing what it is programmed to do. Matzah made by hand, however, is done with the intent of facilitating fulfillment of a divine commandment. Such matzah is preferable for Passover consumption.

Rabbis opposed to machine-made matzah also make a compelling economic argument. Poor families often find extra work in the month before Passover helping bakers prepare matzah by hand. To use machines deprives them of the extra money they need to celebrate the holidays with their families. Many families today choose to purchase handmade matzah if they can afford it. For those who cannot, machine-made matzah is permitted and fulfills the commandment of consuming matzah. Handmade matzah is known as *shmura* matzah, indicating that it has been closely observed and made by hand. Such matzah is typically marked *shmura* on the box.

Matzah typically becomes available about a month before the Passover holiday begins. You can purchase it at most grocery stores or order it online. You can also order matzah from Israel, providing a tangible expression of the link between the Passover meal and the Jewish homeland. There is nothing wrong with eating matzah throughout the year. The only time it is obligatory, however, is on the first night of Passover.

Why do we *have* to eat matzah on that first night? Because having a set time to observe Passover and remember the Exodus makes it much harder to forget or give excuses for why we cannot do it. We celebrate marriages, for example, on the anniversary date. Dedicating one day to it—a day known far in advance—makes it harder to ignore. The same principle applies in daily pursuits we know are important. I have a fixed time for writing every day. If I didn't have it, I could easily be distracted by other things. If we didn't have a set time for eating matzah every year, we might not do it. We need to set aside and fix the times for the most important things in our lives.

A second key symbol is the roasted shank bone, known in Hebrew as the *zeroah*. The shank bone reminds us of the sacrifice of the paschal lamb that occurred during biblical times. The word *zeroah* also echoes the Exodus story. In addition to meaning "shank bone," *zeroah* also means "outstretched," and refers to the outstretched arm with which God delivered the Israelites from Egypt.

The protocol surrounding the shank bone is strict. We are not supposed to point at or lift it up when explaining it. The danger in doing so is that we might suggest we are dedicating it as a sacrifice to God. A little history explains why this is dangerous. With the destruction of the Temple, the practice of sacrifices ceased. In order to renew Judaism and allow it survive after this horrific event, the rabbis had to draw a strict line between the Temple and post-Temple period. The Temple period was over. To even suggest the possibility of making a sacrifice in the modern era borders on heresy. Yet, many Jews still yearned for the Temple in the aftermath of its destruction. Indeed, historians suggest that for hundreds of years after the destruction of the Temple, people would still prepare lamb that resembled the original paschal lamb for consumption at a seder. To discourage this custom, the sages created this law. It may seem overly stringent and unnecessary today, since the offering sacrifices in the Temple ceased almost two thousand years ago. Yet, its persistence teaches us about the power of religious symbolism and wrenching difficulty the first- and second-century Jewish sages faced in surviving after the destruction of the Temple. Because the Temple remained a potent symbol of God's presence, the sages could not prevent all references to it. Yet, were it again to become the focal point of Jewish life, destruction might well follow.

The sages learned this lesson with the failure of a revolt against the Romans in 131 CE. Led by a charismatic leader named Baruch Bar Kochba, who sought to force the Romans out of Jerusalem and rebuild the Temple, the rebels were crushed by the Roman Empire. Scholars estimate that about one third of the Jewish people were killed during the war and the persecution that followed. Revolting and rebuilding the Temple remained an impossibility. Thus, in order to preserve Jewish culture and avoid another tragedy, the sages designated the home and the synagogue as the centers of Jewish life.

The Temple became a "Paradise Lost," a memory of what once was but would not be again for the foreseeable future.

Christians did not face this same difficulty with regard to the Temple's destruction. In fact, writers of the Gospels and later church theologians understood the Temple's destruction as fulfilling the prophecy of Jesus. The sacrifice of Jesus replaced the sacrificial offerings of the Temple. It made atonement for the sins of the world in the same way the sacrifices at the Temple atoned for the sins of Israel.

The destruction of the Temple also helped resolve a lingering debate within the earlier community of Christians. All the earlier Christians had been raised and saw themselves as Jews. They debated whether to reach out and share their message with Gentiles. Many opposed such evangelism. Religious identity in Judaism had always been a matter of birth, as it is still is. Yes, people can convert into Judaism, but that was not a common practice during the first century. Some followers of Jesus urged reaching out to Gentiles as a way of spreading their message. The more traditional members of the community opposed it, arguing for the traditional definition of Jewish identity and pointing to the requirements of circumcision and dietary laws as impossible barriers.

When the Temple was destroyed, the evangelistic point of view gained greater influence. First, the traditional Jewish leadership, who opposed the outreach plan, was weakened, as they had been embroiled in conflict with Rome and amongst themselves. Secondly, some followers of Jesus interpreted the destruction of the Temple as a providential sign that the ancient covenant with Israel was no longer in force. Known later as supercessionist theology, this group argued that God had formed a new covenant based not on biology but on faith in Jesus. This covenant of faith was open to anybody. Third, some historians argue that the move to open up this new group of Jewish Christians to Gentiles served a political purpose. By broadening the base of support, this new movement would face less harassment from Roman authorities. The Jewish faith in one

God had always sparked fascination and intrigue among Roman pagans, but the high barriers of entry made it seem forbidding. The new movement of Christianity offered that same monotheism without the physical and biological barriers of entry. Thus, it began to spread. The destruction of the Temple, then, became not a tragic moment in Christian history. It became a transformative one. At a Christian seder, the shank bone can serve as a reminder of our shared origins and this important historical moment.

KARPAS

The next item on the seder plate is a vegetable we dip into salt water. Celery or parsley is typically used, though the only requirement is that the item be a vegetable. Some families use a potato or an onion. Regardless of which vegetable is used, this dipped veggie is called *karpas*. Scholars suggest the Hebrew word *karpas* comes from the Greek word for vegetable, *karpos*. It may also derive from the Persian word *karafs*, which refers to a plant from which salad is made. There is a biblical reference to *karpas*, but it has a very different meaning. Found in the first chapter of the Book of Esther, it means a "white linen" (1:6). The Talmud uses the word *karpas* in reference to a fine wool. There seems to be no obvious connection between these two usages.

The eleventh-century biblical commentator Rashi, however, draws a connection. Rashi links the Exodus story to the biblical meaning of *karpas* in his commentary on Genesis 37:31-36, the scene in which Jacob's sons convince their father that their brother Joseph has been devoured by a wild beast. This story was the one they told their father to hide their crime of selling Joseph into slavery. To deceive their father, the brothers show Jacob the coat of many colors he had given to Joseph—known in Hebrew as the *ketonent passim*—which they had dipped in blood. They told their father it was Joseph's blood on the coat. Rashi explains the meaning of *ketonet passim* as "*keli milat karpas*," which means a garment made out of fine wool, used for covering a body. Rashi, thus, has drawn an explicit connection between the selling of Joseph into slavery and Passover through the word *karpas*.[1] If this connection feels like a stretch, consider this: the selling of Joseph into slavery is the first step in the story of the Israelite journey to Egypt. That journey leads to slavery and then to the Exodus. By connecting the celebration of freedom with the initial sale of Joseph, Rashi is connecting the beginning and end of the Exodus story.

The custom of dipping the *karpas* in salt water serves several functions. First, the act itself is meant to stimulate interest among children. It sparks one of the four questions asked by the children later in the meal. (See chapter 6.) Seeing the participants dip the parsley into the water, according to this interpretation, causes children to ask why everyone is doing it. The adults answer them through the retelling of the Passover story. The parsley, in other words, is the spark for the story of Joseph. The salt water into which the *karpas* is dipped also symbolizes the tears shed by the Israelites during slavery. The *karpas may* also represent springtime. The green vegetable typically used captures the color of spring.

The ritual and symbolism of the *karpas* stand out for me because of a particular Passover meal. It was my senior year in college. In the fall I had decided to apply to rabbinical school. My relationships with the rabbis I knew and the community-building I had done on campus had convinced me it was the right vocation. I felt a call—a call to serve God and the Jewish people. I knew rabbinical school was competitive, but I was at Stanford University! I had a 3.7 GPA. I had some of the country's most prominent rabbis as my recommenders. My interview felt like a breeze. Friends were giving me sug-

---

1. Rashi on Genesis 37.

gestions on where to live in Jerusalem, where all rabbinical students spend their first year of seminary.

A few days before Passover, I got a letter in the mail. It was in a thin envelope. The letter said I could not be admitted to rabbinical school at this time. I needed to find a job in the Jewish community, work for at least a year, and then reapply. I could never recall feeling as devastated as I did then. I felt rejected—rejected by my community, rejected from the opportunity to do what I knew I was supposed to do.

After a few days the initial devastation wore off. My family and friends rallied around me. At the Passover seder at my parents' house, which I led, I tried to set aside the sadness and experience the joy of the holiday. I got as far as the *karpas* before breaking down. Dipping the parsley in the salt water recalled for me the tears I cried on getting the letter. Yet, the springtime and rebirth it symbolized gave me a kernel of hope. As the seder went on, I knew it would get better. I knew even more in my heart that serving God was my calling, and the seminary would come to see that. The tears of pain had started to give way to the hope of spring. Having just completed my ninth year as a rabbi, I think back to that moment every time I dip the parsley in the salt water.

CHAROSET

Among many participants' favorite Passover foods is *charoset*. This Hebrew word describes a mixture of fruit, nuts, and spices. During the seder, it is combined with the bitter herb to make a sandwich. *Charoset* can be prepared in many ways. Different Jewish communities often develop a unique mixture incorporating local spices or cooking styles. Greek and Turkish Jews, for example, use apples, dates, chopped almonds, and wine. Some communities add coconut. Many families have developed their own *charoset* recipes, and

Passover cookbooks contain numerous options. *Charoset*, unlike the bitter herbs, was not part of the biblical observance of Passover. It became part of the Passover meal during the first century. As a result, it does not have a special blessing associated with it.

Charoset does, however, have an important symbolic role. It represents the mortar the Israelites used to make bricks when they were slaves in Egypt. Mortar is sticky, as is *charoset*. It can also have a chalky texture, as *charoset* typically does. The *charoset* is derived from the biblical Hebrew word *cheres*, which means "clay." Even though the *charoset* symbolizes the mortar of slavery, it tastes sweet, representing the gift of freedom enjoyed by the participants in the seder meal. In effect, *the charoset represents the bittersweet parts of life.*

The *charoset* also has a hidden meaning not mentioned during the seder meal. The reasons for its absence are unclear, but some scholars connect *charoset* with the biblical book known as the Song of Songs. Beginning in the Middle Ages, it became a custom to read or sing the Song of Songs at the conclusion of the Passover seder. Jewish sages interpret the Song of Songs as depicting the love between God and the people of Israel. God's deliverance of the Israelites from Egypt was the greatest expression of that love. The connection with *charoset* comes from the various fruits and nuts described in the book. The verses are as follows:

> Sustain me with raisin cakes, / strengthen me with apples. (2:5)
>
> Your loving is sweeter than wine! (1:2)
>
> His cheeks are like fragrant plantings, / towers of spices. (5:13)
>
> The green fruit is on the fig tree. (2:13)
>
> To the nut grove I went down. (6:11)

These verses each contain fruits or nuts. They can all be used to make *charoset*. The sweetness of *charoset* captures the sweetness of the lovers in the Song.

According to the foremost rabbinical sage of the first century, Akiba, the Song of Songs is an allegory depicting the love between God and the people of Israel. It is, in effect, a sacred love poem.[2] While this allegorizing may seem strange or surprising to some, it fits with a metaphor used throughout the Old Testament. The metaphor is marriage. The relationship between God and Israel is like the one between a husband and wife. The marriage was sealed at Mount Sinai with the giving of the Torah. The metaphor is used by the prophets Jeremiah, Ezekiel, and Isaiah. The Song of Songs is simply reflecting an idea familiar to the Israelites. The metaphor of marriage also reflects the Jewish idea of monotheism. Marriage is the one relationship that demands absolute fidelity to one person. The Jewish people have absolute fidelity to one God. Thus, the relationship between husband and wife is the best metaphor we can use to symbolize it. Religious fidelity is marital fidelity.

For Christians and Jews, reading or studying the Song of Songs on Passover can be a wonderful exploration of the power and meaning of love. Love is Jesus' primary commandment, and the Song of Songs can be interpreted as the love between God and humanity. It can also remind us of the underlying, universal themes behind the Passover holiday. Passover is about more than saying the right prayers and singing the right songs. It is about experiencing the love God felt for humanity and which God expressed by freeing the Jewish people from Egypt.

2. See the article "Song of Songs" in *Encyclopedia Judaica*, vol. 15 (Jerusalem: Keter Publishing House; New York: Macmillan, 1971–1972) col. 144–152.

For Christians and Jews, reading or studying the Song of Songs on Passover can be a wonderful exploration of the power and meaning of love. Love is Jesus' primary commandment, and the Song of Songs can be interpreted as the love between God and humanity. It can also remind us of the underlying, universal themes behind the Passover holiday. Passover is about more than saying the right prayers and singing the right songs. It is about experiencing the love God felt for humanity and which God expressed by freeing the Jewish people from Egypt. Our obligation as human beings and people of faith is to trust in that love and, like the Israelites, let it guide us to the next step on our journey.

MAROR

The fifth symbol is the bitter herb, known in Hebrew as the *maror*. It symbolizes the bitterness of slavery. In the Bible the bitter herb is consumed with the paschal lamb. According to Exodus 12:8, they are eaten together. When the Temple was destroyed in 70 CE, the sages kept the practice of eating the bitter herb, even though they no longer had the paschal lamb. During this period, romaine lettuce typically served as the bitter herb. Even though it does not always taste bitter, lettuce begins by being sweet and ends by tasting hard and bitter. The same change happened while the Israelites were in Egypt. What began with the sweetness of freedom ended with the harshness of slavery. For the last five hundred years, the custom has been to use horseradish, which was the most readily available bitter herb in eastern Europe. Some families place both on the seder plate.

If Passover celebrates freedom, why do we eat something to remind us of the bitterness of slavery? The first reason is empathy. During the seder meal, we are supposed to imagine that we ourselves—not just our ancestors thousands of years ago—were slaves in Egypt and that God freed us and led us to the Promised Land.

Eating the bitter herbs makes the experience more real. *All of us are actors in the drama of the Exodus. In order to play our role well, we need to taste and feel as much of the experience we are reenacting as we can.* Tasting the bitter herbs helps us in this process.

It also reminds us of the contemporary resonance of the Passover theme. When we eat the bitter herbs, we awaken our conscience to the bitterness oppressed people around the world experience today. Tasting the bitter herbs not only creates a bridge to the past but also to the others in the present. In other words, we bring the past to bear on the present.

The deeper lesson of tasting the *maror*, however, is not just to empathize. *Maror* also symbolizes the best way to respond to tragedy and suffering. At the Passover seder we do not take the *maror* and weep over it. We do not engage in self-pity or blame. Rather, we bless it. Consider how audacious an act this is! We bless the symbol of our suffering. This act embodies deep psychological wisdom. We can choose how we respond to tragedy. It is easy to turn inward. It is tempting to focus on what is wrong. Yet, by blessing the *maror, we look for what we can learn from suffering.* Saying a blessing over the *maror* refocuses our thinking. We may not control what happens to us, but we can choose how we respond. By choosing how we respond, we can affect the final outcome. Because the Jewish people did so—because they wrested a blessing out of their suffering—we are all able to celebrate the Passover today.

BEITZAH

The sixth seder plate symbol is the egg, known in Hebrew as the *beitzah*. Unlike the other items on the plate, the egg does not serve a ritual purpose. The only commandment related to the egg is to have it on the seder plate. Its origins lie in the ancient practice of offering a second sacrifice on Passover in addition to the paschal lamb.

Despite its lack of use during the meal, it serves several symbolic functions. Among them are the ideas of rebirth and spring, the evolution of a people, and mourning for the Temple.

Both biologically and culturally, the egg symbolizes the beginning of life. Its connection to springtime, when the natural world renews itself, is obvious. Spring is the time of rebirth. The egg on the seder plate represents the holiday's connection with this season. But the symbolism of rebirth goes even deeper. *The Exodus from Egypt represents the birth of the Jewish people as a nation.* A clan of seventy had traveled from Canaan to Egypt. A nation of over a million people return from Egypt to Canaan. Many nations are born out of persecution. Think of America's Founding Fathers, who forged a unified people in the face of British imperialism. Sometimes persecution can unite a people in a way no other force can. It gave birth to the Jewish people.

The egg represents another part of the Israelites' history as well. The production of an egg does not guarantee that a functioning animal will be born. An unhatched egg is potential life. It is a precondition for life, but not life itself. For the Israelites, the Exodus from Egypt was a precondition for their vitality as a people. They were free, but they did not yet have a purpose. That purpose came seven weeks later with the giving of the Torah at Mount Sinai. Once again, the analogy with America proves instructive. After the Revolutionary War in 1776, Americans were free. They were no longer subjects of England. Yet, it was not until the Constitution was ratified in 1789 that America became a nation with a central government and set of laws. This truth explains why the egg is on the plate, yet it is not used during the meal. The egg represents the first step toward freedom. Yet, we only see its importance in the context of what follows. Becoming a free people is a multistep process.

Jewish tradition later developed another understanding of the egg. For the sages who lived after the destruction of the Temple, the egg symbolized their mourning for it. In Judaism, an egg is the first item served to a mourner after a funeral. In this way, it combines life and death and helps us continue to live when a loved one dies. The egg on the seder plate symbolizes the vitality of Judaism even when the Temple no longer stands.

Symbols matter in religious life. In fact, they matter everywhere. When we use special china at home—when we pour a drink into a particular glass—we recognize the power of symbols. That is the message of this chapter. The ritual foods on the seder plates connect the events of the Bible to the meal we have today. They bring the past into the present. You can travel to a seder in any part of the world and see these same foods. When you know what ritual foods symbolize and mean, they speak more intimately to you. They helped me greatly through a difficult experience in life. If we embrace them with our hearts and minds, they can do the same for all of us.

CHAPTER 6

BLESSING AND QUESTIONING

The Seder Begins

When I played competitive tennis, serving was not my strong suit. Walking up to the baseline made me nervous and uptight. To help develop comfort and ease, my instructor told me to take the following steps: Pick up the tennis ball. Bounce it twice. Pull my racquet back. Toss the ball in the hair. Stretch my arm. Move my racquet forward, making contact with the ball with my arm stretched to its highest point. I followed this precise order with every serve. It did not feel right doing it differently. All rituals work this way. They introduce a measure of regularity into a life filled with uncertainty. We all have them. Perhaps we brush our teeth, wash our face, take off our contacts, and get into bed each night in the same order. Perhaps we drink a glass of water first thing in the morning, then pray, or read, or listen to music. A ritual is simply a series of actions done in a prescribed order on a consistent basis.

In the religious realm, ritual takes on even greater importance. It brings order to the universe. It brings transcendent meaning to the acts we perform. Saying a blessing before a meal differs, for example, from saying "Thanks, Mom" or "Thanks, Dad." It is both a horizontal and vertical act: horizontal in connecting us to others who are also saying a grace before a meal and vertical in linking us with a being, a force in the universe, larger than ourselves. It reinforces the sacred value of gratitude. It gives us a way of looking at the universe as a gift from God.

The Passover meal is filled with ritual. The ritual is so precise that someone in Nashville, Tennessee, could go to a Passover meal in South Korea and feel comfortable knowing what is happening and what will come next. We might think this concern with order limits our imagination. Is there space to experience God? Yes! The order need not stifle our spirits and imagination. Rather, it gives us a framework. It separates our sacred meal from daily life. It gives us a space to sing, teach, laugh, shed tears, and experience God in the ancient traditions of the Jewish people. As we prepare to experience each step of the seder, try to imagine the millions of people who have participated in a Passover seder for thousands of years. You are connected to them, following in their footsteps and adding your voice. As you walk through this chapter, you will understand each act and, I hope, encounter the holy in a new way.

BLESSINGS

Blessed are you, Eternal God, Sovereign of the Universe, Creator of the Fruit of the Vine.

Baruch Atah Adonai Eloyanu Melech Ha-olam Borei Pri Hagafen.

בָּרוּךְ אַתָּה יְיָ אֱלֹהֵינוּ מֶלֶךְ הָעוֹלָם בּוֹרֵא פְּרִי הַגָּפֶן

The seder begins with blessings. A blessing infuses a sacred dimension into what we experience. Blessings also animate life, as we know from the creation narrative, where God creates and then blesses the animals, crops, and human beings. The first blessing in the seder is over the festival wine. In Judaism wine is a symbol of holiness. This particular blessing is called a *kiddish*, a Hebrew word that means "set apart," or "sanctified to God." Through the kiddish blessing, the wine becomes holy. This process models what happens during the Eucharist. The words of the blessing are "Blessed are you,

Eternal God, Sovereign of the Universe, Creator of the Fruit of the Vine." We then drink the first glass of wine.

Saying this blessing, however, does not just sanctify the wine. It also sanctifies the *time*. A Jewish blessing marks a certain time as set apart for holy activity. It thanks God for the opportunity to make this time sacred. This same theology applies to every Jewish holiday. We begin by saying a blessing that sets apart this time as sacred. The logic flows from the story of creation, where the Bible tells us that God rested on the Sabbath, blessed the day, and thereby made it holy. We model God by making time holy.

Blessed are you, Eternal God, Sovereign of the Universe, who has given us life, sustained us and enabled us to reach this momentous occasion.

Baruch Atah Adonai Eloheinu Melech HaOlam shecheyanu v-key-manu v'higianu laz'man hazeh

בָּרוּךְ אַתָּה יְיָ אֱלֹהֵינוּ מֶלֶךְ הָעוֹלָם, שֶׁהֶחֱיָנוּ וְקִיְּמָנוּ וְהִגִּיעָנוּ לִזְמַן הַזֶּה.

The next blessing is one that links the holy time with wonder and gratitude. Known as the *shecheyanu*, it is the blessing that acknowledges the good fortune we have to be alive and experiencing this moment. It asks us to pause and think of all the forces that conspired to bring us to this time. Whenever I say this blessing, I try to remember how interdependent life is. I have arrived at this particular point because of what I did, because of what others did, and because of what God

Known as the shecheyanu, *it is the blessing that acknowledges the good fortune we have to be alive and experiencing this moment.*

בָּרוּךְ אַתָּה יְיָ אֱלֹהֵינוּ מֶלֶךְ הָעוֹלָם, שֶׁהֶחֱיָנוּ וְקִיְּמָנוּ וְהִגִּיעָנוּ לִזְמַן הַזֶּה.

allowed to unfold. When we recognize this truth, we grow in compassion and humility.

One of my favorite Jewish philosophers, Abraham Joshua Heschel, saw wonder as the root of faith. According to Heschel, sin reflects indifference to the world, rather than compassion for and appreciation of it. It arises when we lose our sense of wonder. A blessing, on the other hand, acknowledges our connection with and wonder at the world. Saying a blessing helps move our mind from indifference to gratitude. When we say this *shechyanu* blessing, we open our hearts and minds to God's presence.[1]

THE NEXT RITUAL STEPS

After these opening blessings, we wash our hands. The custom may have begun for reasons of hygiene. Yet, it also serves as a way to prepare our souls. Washing plays a large role in Jewish and Christian tradition. The practice of baptism, for example, began with the Jewish practice of purifying our bodies as a way of showing commitment to God. Before the Passover meal, we seek to prepare our hearts and cleanse our souls by washing.

Next we pick up the parsley from our seder plates. We see its bright green color and think of spring. We hold it between our fingers and dip it into the salt water. In the previous chapter we noted the symbolic importance of this act. The dipping reminds us of the selling of Joseph into slavery that led to the Israelite journey to Egypt and ultimately the Exodus. We noted that the salt water represents the tears the Israelites shed during slavery. We did not note, however, the blessing that accompanies the dipping. As we dip we say the words, "Blessed are you, Eternal God, Sovereign of

---

1. To learn more about Abraham Joshua Heschel, I recommend his book *I Asked for Wonder: A Spiritual Anthology* (Nashville: Crossroad, 1983).

the Universe, Creator of the Fruit of the Earth." Saying a blessing expresses gratitude, but it also asserts human responsibility. We are about to consume something that belongs to God. As the psalmist wrote, "*The earth is the* LORD'*s* and everything in it" (24:1, emphasis added). If the earth belongs to God, what right do we have to take from its produce? We do not own it. In our case, if all the water and vegetables in the world belong to God, how can we take the parsley and dip it into salt water and consume it?

Here is where a blessing makes all the difference. In Judaism saying a blessing is a way of receiving permission from God. When we invoke a blessing over a ritual item, we effectively request God's permission to use it. Its use and fate become our responsibility. If we do not say a blessing, we are essentially committing theft. The Jewish sages put it this way: "It is forbidden to enjoy anything of this world without a blessing, and whoever enjoys anything of this world without a blessing commits sacrilege. Rabbi Judah added: To enjoy anything of this world without a blessing is like making personal use of things consecrated to heaven."[2]

Saying a blessing gives us permission to use something belonging to God. Still, we cannot use it any way we please. We have to use it in accordance with its owner's (God's) laws. Thus, when we say a blessing over the *karpas*, we become responsible for using it in the appropriate way. In our case, it is dipping and eating it and ingesting its spiritual meaning.

We reach now the first thing we do only on Passover: the breaking of the middle Matzah. Earlier we discussed the reason for having three pieces of matzah on the seder plate. Two symbolize the double offering the Israelites made at the Jerusalem Temple on the holidays. The third represents the obligation to eat matzah on the eve of Passover. But why does tradition tell us to take the middle matzah

---

2. Babylonian Talmud, Tractate *Berakot*, 35a.

and break it in half? Why is it also customary to take one half of that matzah and hide it so that the children can look for it after the meal?

The unique name used to describe matzah in the Talmud hints at one of the reasons we break it in half. The Bible describes matzah as the "bread of affliction." That means "the bread of a poor person."[3] Breaking it in half is an act of empathy. One of the horrific realities of poverty is often not knowing where your next meal will come from. A poor person might well divide a small meal so that he or she does not starve later. Dividing the matzah symbolizes the fear that forces people to not eat enough to satisfy their hunger. An impoverished person lacks freedom. In contrast, as we will see later, the ability to share—even a little—is a sign of true freedom.

> *The unique name used to describe matzah in the Talmud hints at one of the key reasons we break it in half. The Bible describes matzah as the "bread of affliction." That means "the bread of a poor person." Breaking it in half is an act of empathy.*

A second reason for dividing the matzah hearkens back to the biblical custom of sacrificing and then eating a lamb on Passover. The lamb was not consumed until the end of the Passover meal and was not to be eaten merely to satiate our appetite. It was meant to be experienced as holy food. Similarly, we save a piece of matzah because it is sacred food, and we do not eat it until after the meal. Hiding it and asking the children to search for it later also helps keep their attention and engagement throughout the evening.

Dividing the matzah into two pieces may also represent the idea that matzah transitions from one meaning to a different one during the seder. At the beginning of seder, before we have told the Exodus story, it is the bread of affliction. It reminds us of the harshness the

---

3. Babylonian Talmud, Tractate *Pesachim*, 116a.

Israelites faced before God redeemed them. By the end of the meal, however, after we have told the story and we have experienced God's redemption, it has become the bread of freedom. As our own situation has figuratively changed, so has the meaning of the bread we eat. By reinterpreting the meaning of the matzah, we highlight our journey from slavery to freedom.

The three pieces of matzah and the breaking of the middle matzah have generated thoughtful Christian interpretation as well. Some Christians see the three pieces of matzah as symbolizing the Father, Son, and Holy Ghost. The breaking of the middle matzah represents the sacrifice of Jesus, who redeems humanity from its broken condition. Some also see the bumpy and sharp texture of the matzah as representing the lacerations and punctures Jesus experienced on the cross.

INVITATION

Passover is a form of communion. It's a meal we eat together. After the middle matzah has been divided and one half hidden away, the leader of the seder issues an ancient invitation. He or she says, "This is the bread of affliction that our fathers ate in the land of Egypt. Let all who are hungry, come and eat. Let all who are needy, come and celebrate Passover. This year we are here—next year, may we be in the Land of Israel. This year we are slaves—next year, may we be free." On the surface, this seems like a simple invitation. Yet, this simplicity hides a deep message. *Sharing is part of being human. It connects us to others. It gives all of us dignity. It affirms our common humanity. Sharing a meal adds to its holiness.*

The opposite of sharing is hoarding. Hoarding is a way of cutting ourselves off from others. A beautiful Jewish teaching on the sins of Sodom and Gomorrah conveys the connection between sharing and dignity. The teaching is found in one of last books of the Talmud known as *Ethics of the Fathers*. The rabbis teach:

> People fall into four types: Those who say, "What's mine is mine, and what's yours is yours"; this is the average, though *some say this is the type predominant in Sodom*. Those who say, "What's mine is yours, and what's yours is mine as well"; this is the fool. Those who say, "What's mine is yours, and what's yours is yours"; this is the saint. Those whose who say, "What's mine is mine, and what's yours is mine"; this is the wicked.[4]

This is a rich text with much to teach. Let us focus, however, on the first sentence. It discusses people who say "what's mine is mine and what's yours is yours." This approach seems normal. Indeed, as the text points out, it's average. Yet, the sages link this normal person to residents of Sodom, who committed grievous sins and were wiped away by God! Sodom is a symbol of human wickedness, and the sages seem to be connecting it to people who simply believe in individual ownership. *The sages are not simply criticizing ownership. They are highlighting the attachment to possessions that cuts us off from one another. They are critiquing the person who becomes a slave to possessions. They are admonishing people who are so wrapped up in themselves that they fail to share any of themselves with others.*

The sages are also offering a moral critique. A culture in which every person thinks only about himself or herself has become dehumanized. It has become much like the one depicted in the popular book and film series *The Hunger Games*. When ownership is everything, we begin to treat people like possessions. That is what the residents of Sodom did. That's what we do when we refuse to give any of ourselves to others. That's what people who have become prisoners to their possessions do. Even if all we can share is a story of pain and suffering, we recognize that suffering shared is suffering

---

4. *Pirke Avot* ("Sayings of the Fathers"), 5:10 (my emphasis).

halved. Beginning the seder by reaching to others begins our own journey to freedom.

We do not only share the meal with others. We proclaim a vision for what our shared destiny will be. The leader says, "This year we are here; next year may we be in the Land of Israel. This year we are slaves; next year may we be free."

This is only the first of the Passover meal's many references to the Land of Israel. We will explore this theme in greater depth in our analysis of the seder's closing verse asking God to help us celebrate Passover next year in Jerusalem.

What unites these two parts of the manifesto—the journey to Israel and the journey to freedom—is the feeling of longing. As people of faith, we have not yet reached the place we are supposed to be. This place is not necessary a geographical location. It is an existential condition. To be human is to be, in some sense, homeless. This truth is why many people view death as a time when we "go home." According to one Jewish tradition, when God created human beings and placed them on earth, they were cut off from their true home, which is heaven.

> *What unites these two parts of the manifesto—the journey to Israel and the journey to freedom—is the feeling of longing. As people of faith, we have not yet reached the place we are supposed to be.*

In this verse the land of Israel symbolizes the idea of our earthly homeland. People without a home are wandering. Having a home helps us feel complete and whole as human beings. It is something we yearn for. The poet Robert Frost captured this yearning when he defined a home as "the place where, when you have to go there, they have to take you in."[5] Israel has always symbolized that home for Jews.

---

5. Robert Frost, *North of Boston* (New York: Henry Holt, 1917), 20.

The final verse invokes the journey from slavery to freedom. It may seem a little strange for us to say "this year we are slaves." We live in a free country. We have the freedom to practice our religion, which is what we do when we gather for a Passover seder. How can we call ourselves slaves? Are we yearning for a freedom we already have?

The definition of freedom envisioned in this verse is global, not individual. It is a world in which individuals are not only free from constraints. It is one in which they have the opportunity to flourish. It is one in which we can live productive and fulfilling lives. Freedom is an achievement that depends upon habits, character, and a sense of responsibility. A person who is not a slave can still lack freedom. Freedom does not depend only on laws and rights. It cannot happen overnight. The world has not yet witnessed it. As Jean-Jacques Rousseau said at the dawn of the Enlightenment, "Man is born free, but everywhere he is in chains."[6] Part of the dream of Passover is that during the upcoming year, we move closer to that state of freedom. The Exodus journey is still not complete. By experiencing the ancient journey of the Israelites, we find the faith to continue it.

FOUR QUESTIONS

Isador Rabi, a scientist who won the Noble Prize in 1944, recalled an insightful story about his childhood. Growing up in a Jewish neighborhood in New York City, he would arrive home from school every day, and his mom would greet him with a question. It was not "how was school today?" or "what did you learn today?" She would ask him, "Did you ask a good question today?" Rabi credits his

---

6. See Jean-Jacques Rousseau, *On the Social Contract and Other Later Political Writings* (Cambridge: Cambridge University Press, 1997), 33.

mother's question with prompting his interest in science and eventual desire to discover something new about the world.[7]

Judaism has always been a tradition that embraces questioning and debate. Questions are a tool for discovering the truth. The most prolific question-askers are our children. Every teacher knows (and sometimes dreads) this truth. Endless questions illustrate a child's desire to learn more about the way the world works. The way we answer those questions shapes a child's experience and understanding of the universe. Through the way we respond to those questions, we can invite our children into our faith and tradition. Their questions open the doors to understanding.

This pattern is modeled during the Passover Seder. Among its most celebrated rituals is the asking of the four questions, traditionally done by the youngest child present. These four questions are ancient. They appear in a text dated to about 80 CE. Scholars also suggest that the four questions were not always presented in the form of questions. Rather, they are one question with four parts. The one question is "What makes this night different from all other nights?" (מַה נִּשְׁתַּנָּה הַלַּיְלָה הַזֶּה מִכָּל הַלֵּילוֹת).

What makes this night different from all other nights?

מַה נִּשְׁתַּנָּה הַלַּיְלָה הַזֶּה מִכָּל הַלֵּילוֹת

This question is followed by four examples of the way the ritual of the Passover meal differs from the ritual of a typical evening meal.

When the Temple stood, the four questions were said after the meal, and not before. The reason is that when the Temple stood, eating the paschal lamb was the central part of the Passover meal, not the telling of the story. After families had completed the highly ritualized

---

7. See *New York Times*, "Izzy, Did You Ask a Good Question Today?" (January 19, 1988), www.nytimes.com/1988/01/19/opinion/l-izzy-did-you-ask-a-good-question-today-712388.html.

meal, the father would prompt the youngest child to ask questions about it. The father would begin this ritual questioning by rhetorically asking the core question of what makes this night different from all other nights. He would then answer his own question, stating the four differences we now pose as questions. This statement of difference was meant to cause the youngest child to ask "why?" The answer to that "why" question would be the retelling of the story of the Exodus. Thus, the four questions were a ritualized way of engaging the children and transitioning from the Passover meal into the Passover story.

This ritualized asking of question remained as part of the Passover meal after the destruction of the Temple. The content was altered slightly, and the questions were given greater prominence in their placement before the meal. The alteration in content was in the fourth question. During Temple times, the final question was "On all other nights, we eat meat that has been roasted, stewed, or boiled. Why tonight do we eat only roasted meat?" When the Temple was destroyed and roasted lamb was no longer part of the Passover meal, this question was replaced with our current one about reclining. *By placing the questions before the meal, the Jewish sages reminded us that the central focus of the evening is not the consumption of the meal itself. It is the telling of the Exodus story.*

The number four occupies great significance throughout the Passover meal. There are the four questions, the four cups of wine, and, as we will see shortly, the four kinds of children. What explains the significance of four?

The answer traditionally given is that the Bible repeats God's promise to redeem the Israelites from Egypt four times. In Exodus 6:6-7, we read:

(1) "I'll bring you out."
(2) "I'll rescue you."
(3) "I'll set you free."
(4) "I'll take you."

This fourfold repetition led the rabbis to incorporate the number four into various aspects of the seder. Another theory, associated with Jewish mysticism, links the number four to the material world. The material world has four directions, four seasons, and four basic compounds (fire, water, earth, air). The nation of Egypt, according to this interpretation, represents the natural world. It is one where might makes right, where corruption reigns, and people are estranged from their deeper spiritual significance. The fourfold promise of redemption represents God's freeing us from the fourfold material world. The Exodus is a journey from the material to the spiritual, from enslavement of the body to freedom of the soul.

The Bible repeats God's promise to redeem the Israelites from Egypt four times.

"I'll bring you out."
"I'll rescue you."
"I'll set you free."
"I'll take you."

Other explanations for the persistence of the number four is that it honors the four matriarchs of the Jewish people—Sarah, Rebecca, Rachel, and Leah. Since Passover is a home-based holiday and the home, in Jewish law, is the traditional domain of the mother, the sages honored the four matriarchs through the continual use of the number. The number four may also be a reference to the four ideological groups in the Jewish community that shaped Jewish belief at the end the first century: the Pharisees, Jewish-Christians, Sadducees, and Essenes. The holiday itself even has four names: *Chag HaPesach* (the festival of Passover), *Chag HaMatzot* (the festival of matzah), *Chag Ha-Aviv* (the festival of spring) and *Z'man Cheiruteinu* (the time of our freedom).

In addition to the four questions, the Haggadah also tells of four types of children. The four children are the wise, the simple, the wicked, and the one who does not know how to ask. The purpose of presenting these four children is clear. *Even two thousand years ago the Jewish sages recognized that people learn differently.* Why these four particular kinds of children? A number of explanations are possible. One I find compelling is that each of these descriptions represents a different stage of a child's development. We begin as the child who does not know how to ask. We are absorbing the world, but not yet asking why it is the way it is. We then become the simple child, developing our curiosity and wonder at the world. We ask many basic questions.

We want to know about everything we see. We are not, however, seeking deep answers. We want to know the basics. As we grow, we may well begin to question what we have learned. Adolescents are famous for rebelling against what they have learned and what their parents claim to know. They want to carve their own path, and the question of the wicked child, "What does this mean *to you?*" captures that feeling of growing independence from what one had learned in childhood. Then, however, with nurturing parents and teachers, we grow into the stage where we want to learn more than just what is true. We seek to learn how things came to be. We want to explore the complexity of the world and the intricate way God designed it. We never fully complete the stage of the wise child. We recognize that learning and gaining wisdom is a process, and not an end state. It is a way of looking at the world. As the Talmud states, "Who is wise? One who learns from all people."[8]

Perhaps the most troubling of the four children is the one referred to as "wicked." The Talmud, in fact, devotes more attention to the wicked child than any other. This extensive focus may indicate the sages' discomfort with this type. How can we call a child wicked? Presumably, since he or she is a child, he or she is not yet fully developed. Wickedness implies a fixed character trait. In literature and film, characters who are wicked generally do not change. To describe a child as wicked—the Hebrew word is *rasha*—makes it seem as if

8. *Pirke Avot* ("Sayings of the Fathers"), 4:1.

Judaism believes that a child can be inherently wicked and without possibility for good.

A possible resolution to this dilemma is found through nuance in the language. The child is described as *rasha*, which can mean "bad" or "wicked." *But the use of the adjective does not imply the existence of the noun.* In other words, the child does not necessarily contain wickedness or evil.

This lesson hit home for me during an unfortunate incident. We had hired a new nanny for our four-year-old son Tam. I will be totally honest—our four-year-old is very high energy. He runs us ragged and exhausts a typical sitter in half an hour. We were excited about the new sitter who was young and active. Then we got home after her first day. Tam was carrying around a piece of paper saying "Tam is a bad boy." He then told us several times that he was a bad boy. In fact, it continued for days. My wife and I were dumbfounded. We told him he was not a bad boy. He may have done something wrong—at this point we didn't really care what it was—but doing something wrong does not make him bad. That was this sitter's first and last day. What Tam did may have been wrong. But it did not determine his character.

Similarly, the fourth child may have behaved in a way that can be called wicked. But that behavior may stem from misunderstanding rather than evil intentions. The child may be ignorant without being malicious. A better translation for *rasha* in this situation would be "wayward" or "mistaken." From this perspective, the wayward son may be compared to the prodigal son described in the New Testament. A child rejects his or her parents' heritage, but retains the possibility for return.

This perspective also helps us understand the response the Haggadah instructs parents to say to the wayward child. The child's question, "What does this holiday mean *to you?*" expresses distance. The child feels isolated and alone, much the same way the prodigal son feels when he begins his journey of return. He even says to his father, "I no longer deserve to be called your son" (Luke 15:21). Yet, his father welcomes him home with compassion. Part of the beauty of the Passover meal is that it brims with the possibility of return. The fact that the wicked child is at the seder and participating indicates hope. The parent's answer in our text may not seem compassionate. He or she says to the child, "Had you been there, you would not have been saved," referring to the God's salvation of the Jewish people in Egypt. Yet, I see that verse as a challenge to the parent rather than a rebuke of the child. No parent should allow a child to feel so alone and isolated that he or she lacks any hope for salvation. The door of return must always remain open. And the parent needs to constantly remind the child of the joy and power of living by faith. Like the prodigal son who "was dead and is [now] alive" so the wicked child may feel removed from the community, but he or she can return again (Luke 15:32).

Thus far the seder has taught us much about Jewish tradition. We learned we create holiness in time through the opening kiddish, which sets apart the Passover day as sacred. We learned that this is an example of the way Judaism sees holiness primarily in time rather than space, as exemplified in God's resting on the Sabbath day and calling it holy. We saw that blessings are the tool through we invoke God's presence and sanctify the ritual items of Passover.

We also saw the way Passover requires our empathy and imagination. During Passover we imagine ourselves as slaves who experienced God's redemption and were freed from Egypt. We invite guests to share the matzah, the simple bread of affliction, illustrating the universal message and meaning of Passover's vision of freedom. From the Jewish perspective freedom is not simply the absence of constraints. It demands responsibility and the means to realize individual and communal fulfillment. That is the journey encompassed in the Passover seder. We begin with the bread of affliction. We then tell the story that transforms it into the bread of freedom.

The way that story is told is meant to provoke interest and questions from the children in attendance. What has provoked you? The Passover meal transforms us by challenging and triggering our senses. The seder itself touches on all of our senses. The ritual items draw our sight. The food reaches our taste buds and sense of smell. We touch the matzah and feel its perforations and imagine the pain of slavery. And we hear the story, the songs, and the prayers. The Passover meal is our journey of the head, heart, stomach, and soul.

CHAPTER 7

"AS THOUGH YOU YOURSELF JOURNEYED FROM SLAVERY TO FREEDOM"

Telling the Passover Story

We can learn a great deal about people by the way they tell stories. Do they tell stories of hope and change? Do they tend to see themselves as victims? Are they optimistic or pessimistic? The stories we tell ourselves also shape our behavior. They give us hope or despair. They can call upon our higher or our lower instincts. A rabbinic mentor once told me to "make up a good story, a noble prevarication, about your congregation and tell it to anyone who will listen. Even if it's not true, after a few years, people will try to live up to it." He captured an essential truth about people. *We live up to the narratives we tell ourselves. We make decisions and act in certain ways because it fits into our story. If we change that story, we can change our lives.*

The same truths manifest themselves in the way a culture tells its stories. For the Jewish people, the Exodus from Egypt is the story of stories. It is the narrative giving us our identity and purpose. The story is told through us. And it is a story of hope and responsibility. It speaks to God's redemptive role in history. It reminds us that we are not at the mercy of impersonal forces or dictatorial rulers. We are children of a God who can and will redeem the faithful.

For the Jewish people, the Exodus from Egypt is the story of stories. It is the narrative giving us our identity and purpose.

The heart of the Passover seder is a lengthy retelling of the Exodus story. My daughter asked me recently why we have to tell the same story every year. She knows the story already. Why we do have to tell it again? Because in retelling the story, we make it our own. We make it our own as a group. And we make it our own as individuals. We see ourselves in it. We look at our own journey, the journey undertaken in each of our lives. And telling the story out loud—not just reading it silently to ourselves—gives it a different kind of power. To simplify this idea, think of the difference between thinking "I love you" or saying it aloud to a spouse or friend. Saying it aloud makes all the difference.

One of the great Jewish mystics, Rabbi Isaac Luria, taught this truth. He argued that the success of the Exodus journey depended on language. Pharaoh sought to separate the Israelites from their language. He used word play to make this argument. In Hebrew the word *pharaoh* can be divided into *Pe-Rah*, which means "evil mouth." Pharaoh, he taught, sought to make the Israelite mouths evil by corrupting their language and forcing them to forget their native Hebrew.[1] This corrupting of language is not unusual when one powerful group wants to eliminate another. In Australia, the English settlers virtually destroyed the Aboriginal people by forbidding their language. Language is powerful because it both expresses our thoughts and shapes the wider culture. Forbidding a language is a way of destroying a culture. If we cannot express an idea, we begin to lose touch with it. The battle in contemporary American culture over religious language is a case in point. It can sometimes feel as if a "language police" monitors people of faith in order to prevent the use of religious language in public.

The Israelites, however, refused to give up their native Hebrew. They did not succumb to Pharaoh's attempt at cultural destruc-

---

1. See Eliahu Klein, ed., *A Mystical Haggadah* (Berkeley: North Atlantic Books, 2008).

tion. In Luria's beautiful phrase, they maintained the "covenant of speech." This commitment warranted God's ultimate redemption and, according to Luria, the Hebrew word *Pesach* captures this idea. Luria pointed out that *Pesach* can be divided into *Peh-Sach*. *Peh*, as we already know, is mouth. Jewish mystics, drawing from insights in Jewish numerology, connect the word *sach* to another Hebrew word meaning "life force." *Peh-Sach, therefore, is the holiday celebrating speech as our life force. Through the telling of our story, we give life to our people.*

EMPATHY

The retelling also evokes empathy. During the seder we are meant not so much to listen to the story, as we are meant to *experience* it. The text of the story frequently uses the first-person plural. Pharaoh enslaved *us*. God freed *us*. Participating in a seder is like entering into a time machine. We are Israelites journeying from Egypt thousands of years ago. Among Jews of Yemenite origin in Israel, it is still customary to dress like the ancient Israelites by wearing the sandals and clothing of nomadic desert-dwelling people!

In every generation, each of us must see ourselves as if we personally had come out from Egypt.

—The Talmud

The Talmud hammers home this point in saying, "In every generation, each of us must see ourselves as if we personally had come out from Egypt."

This aspect of the seder—that it is a reliving in the present, not just a retelling of the past—is part of what makes it relevant to contemporary Christians. The Passover story is not just a part of Jewish history. It delivers a universal message of hope. In this sense, it is similar to the celebration of Thanksgiving. We may not be directly related to the Pilgrims who shared the first Thanksgiving meal with Native Americans in what would become Massachusetts. Yet, we are their spiritual descendants, expressing gratitude for our sustenance, our family, and our country. Jews and Christians are both spiritual descendants of those who experienced the Exodus from Egypt and saw God's redemptive power. Their story is our story. We see ourselves in their story and can draw truths from it. Among the truths we can draw from the Exodus story are that the past can illuminate the present, God works in history, and we are part of something larger than ourselves.

THE PAST IS PRESENT

The Exodus story does not begin in Egypt. It begins in Mesopotamia with a man named Terach, the father of Abraham, who was the father of the Jewish people. We read that Terach was an idol worshiper, and his son Abraham rejected his father's practice and began a new people dedicated to belief in one God. The Haggadah retells this story, describing Abraham traveling from Mesopotamia to Canaan and Egypt, and his grandson Jacob later following in his footsteps. Jacob and his children eventually settle in Egypt, as we know, and became a nation there. They experience four hundred years of slavery until God redeems them.

Focusing much of this early part of the Exodus retelling on the life of Jacob, the sages who compiled the Haggadah were revealing much about their understanding of themselves. They identified with Jacob. They lived in the first and second centuries of the Common Era. It was one of Roman domination. The Roman Empire ruled the ancient Near East and had crushed the Jewish community that challenged its rule in 70 CE. The Romans frequently targeted Jews and Christians and often forbade the teaching of their traditions and community gatherings. The Jewish sages viewed Rome in the same way they viewed Egypt, although they could not state this view overtly for fear of greater persecution. Instead, the rabbis taught this truth through interpretation and biblical symbolism. The symbol for Rome was Jacob's brother Esau. The Bible describes Esau as a hunter and outdoorsman. He was much stronger than Jacob. He threatened several times to kill Jacob. Yet, God assured Jacob of his protection and survival. All of us identify with different biblical characters. Their struggles become our struggles. The Jewish sages looked to Jacob. He faced persecution. He relied on God's promise to deliver him. So did the ancient Israelites. In focusing the early part of the Haggadah on Jacob, the sages are drawing from the past to understand the future. They are the descendants of Jacob fighting the Romans, the descendants of Esau.

In one beautiful interpretation of a famous biblical story, the rabbis express this fear of Rome and concomitant faith in God's protection. The story is Jacob's dream of a ladder between heaven and earth. The ladder, the text tells us, was filled with angels rising and descending upon it. The rabbis compared the angels to the powerful nations of history. Egypt rose, and it fell. Babylonia rose, and it fell. Persia rose, and it fell. But, the rabbis then ask, what will happen with Rome? It has risen. And it does not seem it will ever descend. "Fear not," God tells them. "Rome, too, will descend." This story expresses the rabbis' trust that Rome would not destroy them. So long as they remained faithful to God, God would remain faithful to them and ensure their survival, just as he did with their ancestors in Egypt.[2] For them and for each of us, faith is a promise of our eternal survival—that our lives are not in vain.

---

2. See James Kugel, *The Ladder of Jacob: Ancient Interpretations of the Biblical Story of Jacob* (Princeton: Princeton University Press, 2009), 21.

GOD IS REAL

Yet, even as God promised Jacob survival, and eventually redeemed the ancient Israelites, why did they have to suffer? My confirmation students ask me variations of this question every year. Why did God allow the Israelites to remain slaves in Egypt for four hundred years? If God had the power to redeem them, why did he not do so earlier? The concern expressed in these questions reflects the core tensions of faith. If God is benevolent and omnipotent, why do bad things happen to good people? Millions of books and essays have been written on this issue. It even has a technical academic name—*theodicy*. Yet, in addressing this concern as it relates to the Exodus from Egypt, Jewish tradition has a clear answer. Norman Lamm, one of the most prolific and respected Orthodox rabbis of the twentieth century, put it this way: "Jacob and his children suffered the yoke of Egypt so they were rewarded with redemption. Their very exile entitled them to the greatest joy known to any nation in human history."[3]

In other words, the Israelites experienced redemptive suffering. They had to pass through the valley of the shadow of death—Egypt—so that they could eventually dwell in the land of milk and honey—Israel. God knew this all along, and the experience in Egypt made the land all the more precious and sacred to the Jewish people.

The deliverance of Israel from Egypt also made God real to the people. It was their first lesson in the meaning of grace. The seminal expression of this grace was God's splitting of the Red Sea. When the Israelites reach the Red Sea, they are utterly helpless. Pharaoh's troops are closing in on them. The waters stand in front of them. Only a miracle can save them. When God produces that miracle, the Israelites' faith is transformed. They take the first step in mov-

---

3. See Norman Lamm, "Bittersweet: Passover Sermon", 1967, available at http://brussels.mc.yu.edu/gsdl/collect/lammserm/index/assoc/HASHb54d.dir/doc.pdf.

ing from a people enslaved to Egyptian idolatry to one guided by God's power. We see evidence for this transformation in their first actions after crossing the sea. The Bible tells us, "Israel saw the amazing power of the LORD against the Egyptians. The people were in awe of the LORD, and they believed in the LORD and in his servant Moses" (Exodus 14:31). For Jews, God's deliverance from Egypt is the supreme

The deliverance of Israel from Egypt also made God real to the people. It was their first lesson in the meaning of grace.

act of grace. It led Jews throughout history to have trust in God's ultimate benevolence.

For the Israelites seeing the splitting of the sea also opened up their hearts and minds in an unprecedented way. God was more real to them than at any other time in history. In some ways all of us who seek a life of faith today are at a disadvantage compared to the Israelites. They saw the sea split. They witnessed a concrete, sweeping example of God's power. None of us have had a similar experience. But we can mine our own lives for examples of God's redemptive power.

At my synagogue we have a practice of asking people to give a testimony or personal expression during major holiday worship. They usually reflect on a major life experience—an illness or a death or a feeling of awe—that opened them up to God. Their testimony not only opens their own hearts. It opens the hearts of all of us who are witnessing their retelling. We discover God living and breathing in our own community.

A VISION OF JUSTICE

During the Passover meal, the story is not told just by one person. It is told by all the participants. Most seders have a designated leader who guides the guests through the story, but each guest reads part of it. This process helps each of us identify with and relate to the story. We also take steps to actively engage the senses as a way to stimulate participants' interest in the story. When reciting the ten plagues, for example, it is customary to dip your finger into your cup of wine and spatter out a drop for each plague. The drops of wine we spill symbolize the tears of the many innocent Egyptians who suffered as a result of the plagues. Many families also use this part of the seder to mention modern experiences of unjust suffering. At my own seder, we mention those people around the world who are prohibited from practicing their religion. We mention the refugees who have been uprooted from their homeland because of violent conflicts. The innocent still suffer, and the tears of the Egyptians remind us of their pain.

Another way many people connect themselves to the seder ritual is adding items to the seder plate. The word *seder* means "order," and the Jewish sages outlined a specific order and set of ritual items for the Passover meal. This order connects all people who observe the seder, giving us a powerful sense of community and service. Within that order is space for flexibility because the Passover message is meant to speak to us here and now. *So long as we do not violate the basic order and themes, we can add prayers and rituals that speak to our present concerns.* This flexibility reminds us that the Passover seder needs to speak to us where we are. It is a living ritual, not a fossil. It is meant for every generation, not just one.

Over the last several decades, many Jewish communities have incorporated new ritual items for the seder plate that broaden the community for whom the Passover message resonates. Here are a few of them:

Miriam's Cup: Moses leads the people on the journey from slavery to freedom. Yet, Moses could not have done it alone. In fact, Moses would not have survived his infancy had it not been for the presence of several women: Moses' mother, Jochebed, and sister, Miriam, hide him into a wicker basket and ensure it floats into safety along the Nile River. The two midwives who were told by Pharaoh to kill all Israelite males do not carry out his order on Moses. And Pharaoh's daughter (who is unnamed in the Bible but given the name *Batya* in the Talmud) pulls Moses from the Nile and raises him as her son.[4] Miriam's cup symbolizes these female heroes of the Exodus story. A cup is a fitting symbol for Miriam because she is associated with water in the Bible. This association is even embedded in her name. The Hebrew word *yam* means "sea," and Miriam leads the Israelites women in song after the crossing of the Red Sea. Jewish tradition associates Miriam with a magical well that accompanied the Israelites through the wilderness and quenched their thirst whenever they needed it. They put this magical well in the same category of miracles as the manna from heaven God sent down for the people and the cloud of glory that led the Israelites on their journey. We remember the extraordinary role of Miriam and the heroism of women during Passover by filling Miriam's cup with water and blessing it during the seder meal.

Potato Peels: During the Holocaust, when more than six million Jews were murdered, many starved to death. They had no means to observe the Passover either. The potato peels symbolize the meager food they had, and the tragic loss humanity experienced during this period. These victims yearned for the redemption we are celebrating.

A beet: For vegetarians who choose not to have meat on their tables, the beet often serves as a substitute for a shank bone. Some also see the beet as a symbol of solidarity with those starving around the world who have to subsist on very little. In Israel the beet became the symbol of the tens of thousands of

---

4. See Babylonian Talmud, Tractate *Sotah*, 12b.

Ethiopian Jews who reached Israel in a state of near starvation throughout the 1980s and 1990s, and whose stomachs were so degraded they were not able to eat much substantive food when they arrived in Israel.

A brick: In the midst of the American Civil War, a Union soldier could not acquire *charoset* for a seder. Realizing the *charoset* symbolized the mortar used to make bricks, the soldier improvised and put a brick on the seder plate. Doing so today helps us remember the heroism of soldiers who maintain their faith during times of war.

An artichoke: An artichoke is a complex vegetable with petals, a thistle and a heart. It can symbolize the diversity of faiths conveyed through Jews and Christians gathering around the table for a Passover meal. It can also represent the diversity of humanity. We come from a variety of backgrounds and places, and the world is only growing more interconnected. We strive to live together under the one beating heart of God.

An orange: In the early 1980s, Professor Susanna Heschel, the daughter of Rabbi Abraham Joshua Heschel, added an orange to her seder plate. She said it symbolized the fruitfulness that results when we include in our struggle for freedom all those who have been marginalized and persecuted. The orange cannot be a navel orange. It needs to have seeds, symbolizing the rebirth and new life we gain when we spread freedom to all people.

Inspired by members of my synagogue, I recently made an addition to my seder plate: chocolate. Fair trade chocolate, to be exact. This addition not only provides a wonderful dessert and a little burst of energy during a long meal but also reminds me to look for where people still remain oppressed. It reminds me to try to live the Passover message in my life. One of the ways I can do so is to put my money where my mouth is: literally! Fair trade cocoa beans are grown on farms that pay decent wages and do not house workers in substandard conditions. It is one way workers can escape the cycle of poverty that cripples much of the world. It seems hypocritical to me to proclaim "this is the bread of affliction" and "let all who are hungry come and eat" and then consume products made by people trapped by poverty. Highlighting this reality and showing one simple way to address it makes the Passover message resonate more clearly.

THE POWER OF STORY

The retelling of the Passover story can continue for as long we wish. Some seders are known to last well past midnight with every part of the story discussed and elaborated upon. The central role given to the story represents an important aspect of Jewish theology. We convey truths not through dogmas or statements of beliefs. These statements of faith do have a significant place in Judaism, but the most profound truths are the ones we convey through story. Great stories capture profound truths. They can make these truths more understandable and appealing as well.

A great Jewish teacher taught this truth through a story. One day, he said, Truth was walking naked through the streets. He looked depressed and forlorn. When people saw him, they turned away in disgust. He turned down an alley. There he saw his friend Story. Story was dressed in beautiful clothing. He had a big smile on his face. He was clearly a popular guy. Truth said to his friend, "Nobody listens to me. I'm depressed and alone." Story replied, "The problem is not with you. It is with your appearance. If you took the time to dress as I do, you would find many friends who would listen to you. If you simply appear the way you are, no one will listen." From then on Truth took the advice of his friend Story. He was welcomed with open arms.[5]

The Passover story conveys a truth about God and humanity. We are not meant to be slaves. God desires us to serve and worship God in freedom. We sustain that freedom with memory, gratitude, ritual, and community. It is through God's grace that we discover our responsibility. And we teach the truth of that grace and responsibility through story.

_____

If story helps make truth more appealing, food makes story more tasty.

Story also needs help. It needs a meal to help it go down. It needs people to share its words. It is no accident that the story centers around a meal. If story helps make truth more appealing, food makes story more tasty. Sharing a story during a meal is a timeless human tradition. Perhaps you have a family story you share at special meals or reunions? Part of the beauty of Judaism and Christianity is that they incorporate food and truth into ritual. Now it's time to take a sampler of those foods.

---

5. See Howard W. Polsky and Yaella Wozner, *Everyday Miracles: The Healing Wisdom of Hasidic Stories* (Northvale, NJ: Aronson, 1989), 47.

CHAPTER 8

PRAISING
AND SINGING

The Seder Concludes

A friend of mine on Facebook has listed as his university "The School of Hard Knocks." This particular friend has not had an easy life. He's been through many job changes and difficult relationships. Yet he has become one of the strongest, most resilient people I know. Because of what he has gone through, very little seems to faze him. The same thing can be said about the Jewish people. Having gone through the Exodus from Egypt and countless other persecutions, they have emerged stronger and more resilient. This truth underlies the first ritual item eaten during the Passover meal. It is an egg. The boiling of the egg makes it hard. The more an egg is boiled, the harder it gets. The same was true for the Israelites in Egypt. The more they were persecuted, the stronger they became, until they gained enough strength to follow Moses and journey to freedom.

That freedom is then celebrated through a delicious meal, the specifics of which vary from household to household. For many families, the Passover meal is like Thanksgiving—there are family favorites, served year after year. My family, for example, always serves matzah kugel—a kind of bread pudding but made with unleavened bread— which, according to family lore, was the very first thing my grandmother prepared for her husband during their first Passover together. We also have matzah ball soup, with the matzah balls always coming from a legendary Jewish deli in Chicago called Kaufman's. Several excellent Passover cookbooks have also been written. The most important requirement for the Passover meal is that no leavened bread be served. It is also customary to avoid serving lamb, since it is associated with the old Passover celebration when the Jerusalem Temple still stood. Jewish tradition forbids the serving of lamb lest participants be led to think a real paschal lamb had been slaughtered and sacrificed for the meal.

Jewish tradition also instructs seder participants to lean comfortably in their chairs. Some families place pillows on the seats to convey a feeling of ease. The custom is modeled on the practice of Roman aristocrats who would lean back as a sign of luxury while dining. At Passover, we former slaves signal our freedom by modeling the posture of Roman nobles. Whatever the circumstances—even if the Jewish people were observing the Passover seder in poverty and fear of persecution—they would lean back as a sign of freedom. A profound faith underlies this gesture. No human being is born to be a slave. God desires our freedom. The custom of leaning comfortably during the Passover meal is a physical expression of Thomas Jefferson's words from the Declaration of Independence: "all men . . . are endowed by their Creator with certain unalienable Rights . . . Life, Liberty and the pursuit of Happiness." During Passover there are no slaves. After Passover, we work to turn that vision into a reality.

We noted in chapter 3 the rabbinic practice of sanctifying the communal meal. The sages took a necessary human activity—eating—and sought to use it as a means for religious expression and fellowship. It is difficult to overestimate the importance of this ritualizing of mealtime. It shaped Christianity, whose early fellowships centered on a communal meal that eventually became the practice of communion. It even finds expression in civic life, where saying grace before meals is a standard practice. Aside from its frequency, what is it about dining that makes it an ideal time for religious activity?

The most powerful answer I've heard to this question comes from a story from a rabbinic colleague. He was participating in a retreat, part of which focused on mindful eating. He and the other rabbis in attendance were told to take half an hour and eat one small box of raisins. They had to use the full half hour to eat the raisins, and not quickly pop them in their mouths. The experience was transformative. He reflected on it later, writing,

> We experienced them one raisin at a time; savoring texture, smell, appearance, taste and even the sound of our own chewing and swallowing. A whole world opened up from a single tiny piece of fruit. And in those moments of awareness, I was all about gratitude for the moment and the gifts. And there was a calm that went with that awareness, and an awe I would never have expected to have felt. If I could bring that awareness to the family meal, how might our discourse and experience and companionship be changed, enhanced, blessed![1]

Both Judaism and Christianity enhance and bless our mealtime through ritual. When we practice it consistently, the results are transformative. We begin to see not only meals but much of the habits and regular practices of daily life as opportunities for holiness. We see this truth in miniature in the traditional observance of Passover because it is not just about participating in a seder. It also includes eight days of extra-mindful eating, where we do not consume any leaven. The seder is

Passover is not just about participating in a seder. It includes eight days of extra-mindful eating, where we do not consume any leaven. The seder is just the beginning. The deeper meaning comes when we bring mindful eating to our everyday lives.

1. Rabbi Rex Perlmeter, "I Am How I Eat," blog post, Union for Reform Judaism (February 17, 2012), http://blogs.rj.org/blog/2012/02/17/how-i-eat-is-what-i-am/.

just the beginning. The deeper meaning comes when we bring mindful eating to our everyday lives.

In addition to being a daily practice, eating is also something we traditionally do at home. Today we dine out more and more. Yet, for most of human history, meals have been eaten at home. The Bible tells us the first Passover meal took place in Israelite homes. The home is where our most important education takes place. It is at home where we learn respect, graciousness, kindness; it is where we learn how to make sacrifices for the sake of others, how to speak, and how to listen. The home is where we learn what makes relationships work or not work, and where we realize we are part of a community bigger than ourselves. What better place to learn and celebrate our faith than at home?

Having Passover at home also makes it an opportunity for hospitality. We discussed the invitation for all those who are hungry to come and eat, which is traditionally stated at the beginning of the seder. It is also a custom for a religious community to ensure every person has a place where they can participate in a seder. Hospitals often host them. Synagogues coordinate invitations for visitors and tourists. The way we treat guests says much about our character. The Jewish sages included hospitality—the Hebrew phrase for it is *hachnasat orchim*, meaning "welcoming guests"—among the ten habits that ensure people a place in heaven.

> *The Jewish sages included hospitality—the Hebrew phrase for it is* hachnasat orchim, *meaning "welcoming guests"—among the ten habits that ensure people a place in heaven.*

It is no accident that the early Christians followed Jewish custom and gathered in one another's homes and created the fellowship that blossomed into the church. Over time, however, Christian observance began to move more toward the church than the home. This development may have emerged during the time when Christianity became associated with the state and political power and its institutional expression in church buildings. The church building became the place where sacraments were offered and where people gathered for worship. While the home has never been unimportant, it is not the center of Christian religious life. In Judaism, however, the home still is.

I often teach this lesson by recalling a conversation I had with a family. The mother and father would constantly apologize to me for not attending Sabbath services on Friday evening, which is the central time for worship in Reform Judaism. They apologized to me so often that I thought they were feeling guilty about something, so I asked what they were doing instead of coming to Temple. "Oh," they said, "we're having Sabbath dinner as a family." I told them I would rather they did that than come to worship! Perhaps a rabbi discouraging worship attendance sounds blasphemous. Yet, these parents knew that what happens in the home shapes their family and expresses their commitment to God and their faith. They were making sacred time during a hectic week, and I applauded and thanked them for it.

THE HIDDEN MATZAH

The first act after finishing the meal is to eat the *afikomon*. This is the broken half of the matzah held up at the beginning of the seder and then hidden for the children to find. The word *afikomon* is the based on the Greek word *epikomon*, which was the after-dinner activity in ancient Greece. In Plato's *Symposium*, it involved visiting friends and drinking. It also refers to dessert. By referring to the hidden piece of matzah as the *afikomon*, the Jewish sages sought to convey several ideas.

First, the *afikomon* serves as a substitute for the paschal lamb. In biblical times the lamb was last thing eaten during the Passover meal. So it is with the *afikomon*. It is traditionally broken up into enough pieces for everyone at the seder to have one. Second, calling this piece of matzah an *afikomon* was a way for the sages to limit the activity on Passover evening. The last taste in our mouth should be one of holiness. In connection with this custom, they also ruled that no other social or intellectual activity can follow the conclusion of the Passover seder. Whereas the Greek symposium could end with drinking and carousing, the Seder ended with matzah and discussion. This difference points out a central contrast between the two formative cultures of the modern world. Hedonism was a viable part of Greek philosophy, expressed in the *Symposium* and other literature. Holiness was the core part of Jewish culture, expressed in the setting aside of the Sabbath day and ritual purity laws described throughout the Bible. One culture diminished after Alexander the Great. The other survives to this day.

A third custom of the *afikomon* is to have children search for it. As we noted in chapter 6, the Seder leader hides the *afikomon* at the beginning of the evening. After the meal is concluded, the children search for it. The Talmud says this custom helps keep the children engaged and awake throughout the evening. Some families turn the searching for and discovery of the *afikomon* into a major event. Rabbi Marc D. Angel, notes:

> It is customary in many Sephardic [Jews whose origins are in Spain and the Middle East] households to wrap the *afikomon* in a sack, and for each participant to have the opportunity to sling it over his shoulder. This is symbolic of the Israelites carrying their burdens as they left Egypt. Some have the custom of actually standing up and walking around the table with the sack on their shoulder. Those present ask: From where are you coming? The

answer is: From Egypt. Then they ask: Where are you going? The answer is: To Jerusalem.[2]

The *afikomon* thus represents the journey from Egypt to the Promised Land. The children at the seder reenact that journey in their search and discovery of it.

After the *afikomon* has been eaten, the after-dinner blessings are sung. Jewish law prescribes a much longer set of blessings to be recited after the meal than said before it. For sages, after dinner was a perfect time to pray and say blessings. Before a meal, we are focused on filling our hungry stomachs. Afterwards we are satiated and ready to thank God for what we have enjoyed. In fact, the Bible specifically commands saying grace after the meal, as we read, "You will eat, you will be satisfied, and you will bless the LORD your God in the wonderful land that he's given you" (Deuteronomy 8:10). Biblical commentators suggest the Bible commanded we say grace after the meal to counter our natural instincts. Once we have eaten, we may forget the pangs of hunger. We may forget how blessed we are to be able to meet our basic needs. *It is when we are likely to forget that we most need to be reminded.* The after-dinner blessings also transform what was a biological necessity into a spiritual affirmation.

> *The afikomon thus represents the journey from Egypt to the Promised Land. The children at the seder reenact that journey in their search and discovery of it.*

> *Those present ask: From where are you coming? The answer is: From Egypt. Then they ask: Where are you going? The answer is: To Jerusalem.*

---

2. Marc D. Angel, ed., *A Sephardic Passover Haggadah* (Hoboken, NJ: KTAV, 1988), 21.

After saying the after-dinner grace, we fill the third cup of wine, bless it, and drink it. Then we tell the story of Elijah the Prophet.

He is one of the most enigmatic figures in the Bible. He appears several times in the First and Second Books of Kings. His most well-known role in the Bible is denouncing King Ahab and Queen Jezebel for immorality and idolatry. He is also one of two figures in the Hebrew Bible who never dies. The first is Enoch, whose life ends when he "walks with God" (Genesis 5:24). Elijah departs the earth in a fiery chariot in 2 Kings 2:11. We do not know where he goes and we do not hear from him again. We do, however, hear *about* him again at the end of the Book of Malachi. Malachi, which is the last of the Prophetic books, ends with the prophet Malachi proclaiming, "Look, I am sending Elijah the prophet to you, / before the great and terrifying day of the LORD arrives" (4:5). The Jewish sages interpreted this verse to mean that Elijah would appear as the precursor to the Messiah, whose presence would usher in the "great and terrifying day of the LORD." John the Baptist in the New Testament serves that precise role. He announces the coming of the Messiah.

Around the same time of the appearance of John the Baptist, the Jewish sages began creating folklore around the figure of Elijah the prophet. Stories of his arriving on earth to fight injustice and perform miracles became well-known. In an expression of hope for his arrival, we leave an empty seat, setting, and full glass of wine at every Passover table. These are reserved for a possible visit from Elijah. In fact, at this point in the seder, it is customary to open the

After saying the after-dinner grace, we fill the third cup of wine, bless it, and drink it. Then we tell the story of Elijah the Prophet.

In an expression of hope for his arrival, we leave an empty seat, setting and full glass of wine at every Passover seder. These are reserved for a possible visit from Elijah.

front the front door to welcome Elijah in case he has been waiting. (Several years ago I conducted a seder near the top of a high-rise building, so we sent the elevator down to see if Elijah had been waiting for it!)

Elijah also adds a new element of time to the seder. We have remembered the past through the retelling of the Exodus from Egypt. We have brought this story up to the present through observance of the seder and the four questions in which the children ask about why we relive this story today. Elijah points us toward the future, giving us hope that tonight might be the night he arrives and heralds the beginning of a new era.

Elijah serves in this role of pointing to the future in another major Jewish ceremony: the ritual circumcision of a baby boy. At every circumcision an empty seat is arranged for Elijah. It represents the child's future. Perhaps he might be the one who leads us into a new era. Perhaps he will live in a world free from violence and persecution.

Elijah's connection to children and families is found in the Bible as well. Elijah, the prophet Malachi said, would "turn the hearts of the parents to the children, / and the hearts of the children to their parents" (Malachi 4:6). In other words, reconciliation among families is a precursor to peace in the world. Without families getting along, how can we expect people of different nations and cultures to live in harmony? Elijah is a paragon of that hope. It is not a blind, passive hope. Elijah urged the Israelites to reject idolatry and return to the core of their faith. When we leave him a seat at the Passover table, we proclaim that this vision is possible. No matter the circumstances, we have not, as the Israeli national anthem proclaims, "lost our hope."

The custom after Elijah's cup has generated much controversy throughout history. It is a condemnation of those peoples who have profaned God's name and persecuted the Jewish people. It asks God to "pour out Your wrath" on such peoples. The controversy emerges because some people interpret it as a call for vengeance. One of the central themes of Passover is God's mercy and compassion, and here we are asking God to wreak havoc on those who have hurt us. Others question its seeming rejection of anyone who does not agree with Jewish beliefs. Did the sages intend for God to hurt all non-Jews? In our day and age, with so much religious hatred, how can we recite such a prayer?

Because of these concerns, some communities eliminate this passage altogether. Others soften its language. I prefer to preserve it because my research suggests neither of these controversial interpretations fits with the text or its origins. The text itself was inserted into the seder during the First Crusade (1096), where scores of Jewish communities were destroyed by invading armies from Europe. This event began a new era of Jewish persecution that culminated in the expulsion of Jews from England, France, and Spain. The communities that inserted this passage in the Haggadah felt the pain of hatred and fear of death. In recalling the Exodus from Egypt, they yearned for a world free of hatred. This prayer is asking God to ensure justice be done in heaven, even as it has not been done on earth. *The prayer is not a call for human acts of vengeance. It is a plea for God to call people to account for their acts of injustice on earth.*

To this end, a sixteenth-century rabbi from Germany added a paragraph to the traditional passage in his Haggadah. It asks God to "pour out Your love" on all those cared and befriended Jews rather than persecuted them:

> Pour out Your love on the nations who have known You and on the kingdoms who call upon Your name. For they show loving-kindness to the seed of Jacob, and they defend Your people Israel from those who would devour them alive. May they live to see the sukkah of peace spread over Your chosen ones, and to participate in the joy of your nations.[3]

---

3. See David Dishon and Noam Zion, *A Different Night, The Family Participation Haggadah* (Jerusalem: Shalom Hartman Institute, 1997), 142–43.

Following this call for divine justice, we take up the theme of gratitude once again in a section of the seder called *Hallel*. The word *Hallel* itself means "praise," and it is the root of the Hebrew word *Hallelujah*. In rabbinic Judaism *Hallel* is a series of Psalms of Thanksgiving chanted at special occasions. It is not chanted after every meal. It is reserved for the after-dinner blessings on Passover and for worship services on other holidays. The extra emphasis on Passover comes from the Psalms' frequent mention of God's role in redeeming the Israelites of Egypt. The worship service taking place in the synagogue on the eighth day of Passover also contains a shortened version of *Hallel*. Jewish tradition views this shortening as a curtailment of joy in memory of the innocent Egyptians who died during the plagues and splitting of the Red Sea. Some communities choose to skip or significantly shorten the *Hallel* section during the seder.

Hallel is followed by the singing of several songs unique to Passover. Among the most beloved of these songs is "*Dayenu*." The word itself means "It would have been enough for us." The song is a description, in chronological order, of the miracles God performed and the gifts he gave to the Jewish people—freeing them from slavery, sustaining them in the desert, giving them the Torah,

Following the call for divine justice, we take up the theme of gratitude once again in a section of the seder called Hallel. *The word* Hallel *itself means "praise," and it is the root of the Hebrew word* Hallelujah.

Hallel *is followed by the singing of songs unique to Passover. Among the most beloved of these songs is "Dayenu." The word itself means "It would have been enough for us." The song is a description of the miracles God performed and the gifts he gave to the Jewish people.*

and so on. After each verse, the community of singers declares "*Dayenu*"—if God had done this and no more, it would have been enough for us. These miracles and gifts add up to fifteen, which is a number rich in biblical resonance. The Bible tells us the priests stood on fifteen steps at the Jerusalem Temple when they sang the Psalms. Fifteen of the 150 Psalms begin with the words *Shir Ha-Ma-ahlot*, meaning "A song of ascending steps." Singing a song of fifteen verses hearkens us back to the psalms sung by the priests at the Temple.

Dayenu conveys a gratitude at odds with the tone of much of the Exodus story. When we read it in the Bible, we encounter the seemingly endless complaints of the Israelites toward Moses and God. They yearn for the foods of Egypt. They build a golden calf when they get impatient for God's presence. They bemoan the bitterness of the water. They believe the pessimistic reports of the ten spies who enter the Promised Land and tell the people to be afraid of the "giants" who live there (Numbers 13). In the wilderness they would have been more likely to say to God, "What have you done for me lately?" rather than "It was enough for us that you freed us from Egypt."

The singing of "*Dayenu*" reframes the Israelite experience in a positive way. Instead of remembering the Israelites' impatience and irritability, we highlight their recognition and gratitude for God's extraordinary generosity. An important psychological principle is at work here. *We become what we remember.* The Israelites who complained endlessly to God and Moses in the wilderness did not make it into the Promised Land. Shaped indelibly by the experience of slavery, they were not prepared for freedom. They maintained a slave mentality, yearning for the comfort and certainty of Egypt and lacking the faith in God's promise and support. Their descendants had to be different. Their freedom depended on fealty to God's laws and trust in God's promise. How could they make sense of their ancestors' constant complaining and backsliding?

Dayenu was their answer. It reimagines the past in the context of the present. If this act seems like a rewriting of history, it is. Yet, the rabbis who wrote this song were not interested in history as an objective scholarly discipline. They viewed the past through the prism of memory. Memory is actively drawing from the past to enrich the present and shape the future. Memory is always selective. Some of the process of remembering is unconscious. Certain events stick out regardless of whether we want them to. Yet, we hold a great deal of power in determining what our memories mean. Through this song, the Israelites choose to remember their past as one filled with gratitude and faith. Their faith would make up for their ancestors' ingratitude, and their faith expressed their gratitude for God sticking with the Israelites even when they seemed to have lost faith.

This song also has a message for all people of faith today. A few years ago Reverend Will Davis Jr., wrote a fabulous book called *Enough: Finding More by Living with Less.*[4] Both its title and its message convey the truths captured in *Dayenu*. God built the world with limits. Our purpose as human beings is not to satisfy our every whim and wish. It is to see life as a gift. When we see it as a gift, we will not take it for granted. We will not waste it or treat it with apathy. Rather, we will unwrap the gift and treat it with care and tenderness. We will treasure it and all the other gifts that come along with it. In the case of Judaism, the gifts God gave us include redemption from Egypt, the giving of the Torah, and the building of the Temple. We even received the gift of the Sabbath, which we can reexperience every week.

Receiving the gift of life implies certain limits. We cannot do everything we want. In Jewish law, for example, suicide is forbidden because ultimately, our body does not belong to us. It belongs to God. God built limits into creation. Jewish tradition tells a story

---

4. Will Davis Jr., *Enough: Finding More By Living with Less* (Grand Rapids: Revell, 2012).

about the creation of the world in which each of the different elements of nature competed for domination. The dry land wanted to shrink the borders of the ocean. Fire wanted to have power over water. Water wanted to cover the earth. God finally said "Enough!" God set limits and gave each of the elements their proper place. Their power was limited by one another. When we sing "*Dayenu,*" we are acknowledging the limits on human power. And we are telling God we understand limits of creation and our responsibility for sustaining it.

CLOSING SONGS

After opening the door for Elijah and singing "*Dayenu,*" we reach the concluding part of the seder. A number of songs became part of the seder over the centuries of its existence. They were not likely part of first several centuries of Passover meals, but they accrued into the seder over generations. This accrual follows a theme in Jewish ritual. A prominent rabbi would add a song or reading to a ceremony, and it would become a standard part of it. Thus, a seder or another holiday celebration brings together readings and songs from many centuries. We will focus here on two of the most popular and meaningful closing songs.

The first is "*B'shanah haba-ah b'yerushalyim,*" "Next year in Jerusalem!" We know from chapter 2 that before the destruction of the Temple in 70 CE, a massive Passover

> *After opening the door for Elijah and singing* "Dayenu," *we reach the concluding part of the seder. A number of songs became part of the seder over the centuries of its existence, among them is* "B'shanah haba-ah b'yerushalyim," *To say* "Next year in Jerusalem" *is to say we aspire for Jerusalem to be at peace. If Jerusalem is at peace, the world will be at peace.*

celebration was observed each year in Jerusalem. It was, by some accounts, the pinnacle of the year. At no other time during the year did as many pilgrims descend on Jerusalem. Through the lens of history, this Passover celebration has come to represent the golden age of Jewish life. It symbolizes a time of freedom, strength, and prosperity. Yet, until 1948, no Jews could live in freedom in Jerusalem. A desire for return to that holy city permeates Jewish prayer and literature. During prayer we face toward Jerusalem. A glass is shattered at the conclusion of every wedding in its memory. Psalm 137 captures this yearning in poignant words:

> Alongside Babylon's streams, there we sat down, crying because we remembered Zion. We hung our lyres up in the trees there because that's where our captors asked us to sing; our tormentors requested songs of joy:
> "Sing us a song about Zion!" they said. But how could we possibly sing the LORD's song on foreign soil? Jerusalem! If I forget you, let my strong hand wither! Let my tongue stick to the roof of my mouth if I don't remember you, if I don't make Jerusalem my greatest joy. (Psalm 137: 1-6)

Saying "Next year in Jerusalem" reflects this hope of return. It proclaims our faith in its eventual realization. The reason we sing it at the end of the Passover seder is that we have just experienced God's redemption of the Israelites from Egypt. Now we pray God will redeem us and the world by allowing Jews to live in peace in Jerusalem. This same hope underlies the story of Jesus' triumphant return to Jerusalem as depicted in the Gospels. This story is so central to Christianity that it is one of the few that appears in all four Gospels. Jerusalem and peace go hand in hand.

We see this even in the word Jerusalem itself. It is the combination of two words—*yir*, which means "city," and *shalem*, which means "peace." Jerusalem is the city of peace. To say "Next year in Jerusalem" is to say we aspire for Jerusalem to be at peace. *If Jerusalem is at peace, the world will be at peace.* If this aspiration seems far-fetched, consider what Jerusalem represents. It is a city central to the world's three major religions. If it experiences peace, so may other parts of the world. Jewish tradition also sees Jerusalem as "a light to the nations," in the prophet Isaiah's phrase (Isaiah 42:6). Peace within the borders of Jerusalem can inspire the world.

So long as that peace has not yet been realized, we still say at the end of the seder "Next year in Jerusalem," even if we are observing the Passover in Jerusalem. I discovered the reason when I was a rabbinical student celebrating Passover there. It was April of 2001. My classmates and I had been in Jerusalem studying for nine months. It had been a terrifying experience. Tensions between Israelis and Palestinians were high; suicide bombings happened almost every week. We were told not to take public transportation or visit any popular tourist destinations. On the first night of Passover we gathered in one of our classmate's house for the seder. It was a remarkable evening, and none of us had ever been in Jerusalem during Passover. Near the end someone got a text message (texting was popular there long before it was in America) with terrible news. A suicide bomber had detonated at a popular hotel in the coastal city of Netanya. He did so in a ballroom crowded with families celebrating Passover. More than thirty people, including several young children, were killed. We were silent, devastated. As we sang "Next year in Jerusalem," tears flowed as we mourned for the dead and yearned for peace in our holy land.

ONE GOAT

After proclaiming a yearning and vision for peace, we conclude the seder with a song seemingly aimed at children and lacking any specific connection to Passover. Entitled "*Chad Gadya,*" which means "one goat," it depicts an escalating chain of disasters that begins when a man purchases a baby goat. The goat is eaten by a cat, which is bitten by a dog, which is beaten by a stick, and so on, until the angel of death is destroyed by God. The closest English equivalents might be "The Farmer in the Dell" or "The Little Old Lady Who Swallowed a Fly." What is it doing in the Passover seder?

According to one popular interpretation, the song is an allegorical summary of Jewish history. The Jewish people are the goat, and everyone wants to destroy them. In the end, only God can save them by vanquishing the angel of death. We sing it on Passover because Passover celebrates God's deliverance of the Jewish people from Egypt. It comes at the end of the seder because it points us to the future deliverance God will bring.

Another interpretation by contemporary theologian Neil Gillman connects the song to the Jewish belief in resurrection of the dead at the end of days. The final verse in which God slays the angel of death refers, says Gillman, to the time when death is defeated and all who lived will come to life again. Its inclusion on Passover is connected to Elijah the prophet, for whom we leave an empty seat at the table and who is the precursor to the end of days.[5]

Other contemporary interpreters see "*Chad Gadya*" as a warning against the cycle of endless retribution. They connect it with a verse from the Talmud in which Rabbi Hillel encounters a skull floating down a river and muses on the way it may have gotten there. "Because you drowned others," he says, "others have drowned you; and in the end, those who drowned you will themselves be drowned."[6] This truth connects with Passover because the Israelites avoided the cycle of retribution in their relationship with Egypt. Even though the Egyptians enslaved them, the Israelites did not seek

---

5. See Neil Gillman, *The Death of Death: Resurrection and Immortality in Jewish Thought* (Woodstock, VT: Jewish Lights, 2000).

6. *Pirke Avot* ("Sayings of the Fathers"), 2:6.

vengeance. Rather, they drew from the experience a lesson about the way to treat outsiders. "Don't mistreat or oppress the immigrant," the Bible teaches us, "because you were once immigrants in the land of Egypt" (Exodus 22:21).

I find this one of the most remarkable lessons of Passover. Instead of hating the Egyptians, we learn from our experience in Egypt to welcome and love the stranger. It is counterintuitive and countercultural. Because of its difficulty, the Bible repeats the admonition to not oppress the stranger thirty-six times. It is not easy, but few of the most worthwhile things in life are.

Thus, with a song of redemption, the seder concludes on a note of hope. The Talmud says in regard to the telling of the Exodus story: "Begin with shame, end with praise."[7] In other words, start with the experiences of pain. End with the realization of joy. And so we do. The Passover meal begins by recounting the bitterness and pain of slavery. We tell that story through ritual, food, and song. And we conclude with the experience of redemption. This ancient experience of redemption gives us hope for today. Just as God redeemed our ancestors, so may he deliver us, wherever we are. This ultimate victory—of life over death—is our eternal promise.

> *The Talmud says in regard to the telling of the Exodus story: "Begin with shame, end with praise." In other words, start with the experiences of pain. End with the realization of joy. And so we do.*

7. Babylonian Talmud, Tractate *Pesahim*, 116a.

CHAPTER 9

FROM ANCIENT ISRAEL TO CONTEMPORARY AMERICA

The Universal Story of Freedom

What about Passover has so captured the imagination of the world? It is the universal story of freedom. Whenever people think of liberty and freedom from oppression, they invariably reference the Exodus story. Its echoes resound to this day because the Passover story is not only a religious story but also a political, philosophical, psychological, and liturgical experience. If it were simply about religion, it would not have inspired people and movements around the world. It would not be among the most familiar stories in the world today. Consider its influence on American history.

The Exodus figured prominently in the imagery of the Revolutionary War and creation of the American government. In 1776, John Adams gave a report from the deliberations of the committee tasked with determining the seal of the United States. Benjamin Franklin, he noted, wanted "Moses lifting up his wand and dividing the Red Sea, and Pharaoh in his chariot overwhelmed with the waters." Jefferson preferred

> *The Passover story is not only a religious story but also a political, philosophical, psychological, and liturgical experience. If it were simply about religion, it would not have inspired people and movements around the world. And it would not be among the three most familiar stories in the world today.*

something a little more subtle. He suggested a depiction of the Israelites wandering through the wilderness with the cloud of fire, representing God, leading them forward. Jefferson also echoed the Exodus story in his second inaugural address. *He compared the Israelites journey to the Promised Land to America's quest to build a new nation.* "I shall need, too," he said, "the favor of the Being in whose hands we are, who led our fathers, Israel of old, from their native land and planted them in a country flowing with all the necessaries and comforts of life."[1]

The connection to the Israelite Exodus shaped not only the American desire for freedom from Great Britain but also drove their self-understanding and vision as a nation. In other words, they understood that the Exodus was not just about freedom. It was also about responsibility. True freedom needed to be sustained by laws and faith. *Freedom from Britain was the Exodus. The ratification of the Constitution was the giving of the Torah at Mount Sinai. God is the thread connecting the two.* It was no accident that Benjamin Franklin chose a biblical verse to be emblazoned upon the Liberty Bell in Philadelphia. "Proclaim liberty throughout all the land unto all the inhabitants thereof" (Leviticus 25:10 KJV).[2] Liberty meant nothing if the people did not appreciate and live by it. The Exodus would have been short-lived without the Torah.

America's founders also had a sense of mission similar to that of the Israelites. God's deliverance of the Israelites was an act not just meant to be heard and appreciated by the Israelites. It was an act of world-shattering importance. It was a message to the nations of the world that no human being is God, and *God does not intend for one*

---

1. Recounted in Forrest Church, *The American Creed: A Biography of the Declaration of Independence* (New York: St. Martins Griffin, 2003). The full text of the second inaugural address is available at http://avalon.law.yale.edu/19th_century/jefinau2.asp.

2. This translation is taken directly from the Liberty Bell.

group to enslave another. Moses notes the global importance of the Exodus when he pleads with God not to destroy the Israelites after they construct an idolatrous golden calf. "LORD, why does your fury burn against your own people, whom you brought out of the land of Egypt with great power and amazing force? Why should the Egyptians say, 'He had an evil plan to take the people out and kill them in the mountains and so wipe them off the earth'?" (Exodus 32:11-12). The Israelites, to quote the Chicago Blues Brothers, were on a "mission from God." What would it say about God if God stopped their journey to freedom after it had just begun?

Many of the early American leaders echoed this missionary language. George Washington did so in his Second Inaugural address. Thomas Jefferson did so eloquently in a 1810 letter, "The preservation of the holy fire is confided to us by the world, and the sparks which will emanate from it will ever serve to rekindle it in other parts of the globe."[3] *America's leaders saw their task as rekindling the flame of freedom first lit by ancient Israel.*

Another group of early Americans also drew inspiration and hope from the Exodus story. Slaves of several generations drew on its imagery, language, and message. One of the most famous spirituals of the Civil War was "Go Down, Moses," picturing Moses pleading with Pharaoh to free the Hebrew slaves. Its key sentence "Let my people go!" is taken direct from Exodus 7:16. It is often included in American seders and has been translated into Hebrew for Passover seders in Israel. Its words also have symbolic meaning. Consider the song in its entirety:

> When Israel was in Egypt's land:
> Let my people go,
> Oppress'd so hard they could not stand,
> Let my People go.

---

3. Quoted in Church, *The American Creed*, 73.

> Go down, Moses,
> Way down in Egypt's land,
> Tell old Pharaoh,
> Let my people go.

Pharaoh and Egypt symbolize the slave master. Israel represents the slaves. Freedom is the ultimate Promised Land. The words "Go Down, Moses" also resonates with the Bible's description of Egypt being a place to which people go "down." From the perspective of the biblical writers, Egypt was below other lands, and was a locale to which people descended. During slavery "going down" was associated with moving farther south along the Mississippi River. The further down one went, the worse conditions became. This song is a plea for God to come down to where slaves suffer and force their pharaohs to set them free.

The often overlooked subsequent verses of the song tell the rest of the Exodus story, connecting freedom through Jesus with the freedom of the Israelite redemption. The last two verses connect the Promised Land to freedom. Freedom from chains of bondage would lead slaves to possess "fair Canaan's land." This one song offers a succinct and inspiring summary of the entire Exodus story.

> "Thus saith the Lord," bold Moses said,
> let my people go;
> "if not, I'll smite your firstborn dead,"
> let my people go!
>
> No more shall they in bondage toil,
> let them come out with Egypt's spoil.
>
> We need not always weep and mourn,
> And wear those slavery chains forlorn.
>
> Come, Moses, you will not get lost,
> Stretch out your rod and come across.

As Israel stood by the water's side,
at God's command it did divide.

When they reached the other shore,
they sang a song of triumph o'er.

O Moses, the cloud shall cleave the way,
A fire by night, a shade by day.

Your foes shall not before you stand,
and you'll possess fair Canaan's land.

This world's a wilderness of woe,
O let us on to Canaan go.

O let us all from bondage flee,
and let us all in Christ be free.[4]

Even though their connection with the Exodus story seems the most obvious and direct, African American slaves were not the only group at the time to draw from the Exodus story. White Confederate leaders did as well. Their pharaoh was the North. Lincoln and his government were oppressing the South by forcing their laws upon it. The war was their fight for freedom. We see this usage in several sermons from white Southern clergymen prior to and during the war. They compare the hardening of Pharaoh's heart with Lincoln's determination to stop secession, and they compare the South to the Promised Land of Canaan.

After the Civil War, the Exodus story continued to resonate in American political and social life, especially among African Americans. During the Civil Rights era, Martin Luther King Jr. drew an explicit

---

4. "Go Down, Moses," *The United Methodist Hymnal* (Nashville: The United Methodist Publishing House, 1989), 448.

connection between the movement he led and ancient Israel through a reference to "Go Down, Moses" in his Nobel Lecture. It reads,

> Oppressed people cannot remain oppressed forever. The yearning for freedom eventually manifests itself. The Bible tells the thrilling story of how Moses stood in Pharaoh's court centuries ago and cried, 'Let my people go.' This is a kind of opening chapter in a continuing story. The present struggle in the United States is a later chapter in the same unfolding story.[5]

King had sounded a similar theme earlier, comparing the *Brown vs. Board of Education* decision forbidding school segregation as the beginning of the parting of the Red Sea. He drew a stark contrast between the fate of those who try to stop the people from crossing and the fate of those who will find freedom from crossing over it. "There is a Red Sea in history that ultimately comes to carry the forces of goodness to victory, and that same Red Sea closes in to bring doom and destruction to the forces of evil."[6] King's reading of the Exodus sees God on the side of the oppressed. It echoes what many throughout history have seen as the story's ultimate lesson.

> *The Bible tells the thrilling story of how Moses stood in Pharaoh's court centuries ago and cried, "Let my people go." This is a kind of opening chapter in a continuing story.*
>
> —*Martin Luther King Jr.*

---

5. See Martin Luther King Jr., "Nobel Lecture: The Quest for Peace and Justice," *Nobelprize.org*, Nobel Media AB 2014, 1964, accessed October 14, 2014, www.nobelprize.org/nobel_prizes/peace/laureates/1964/king-lecture.html.

6. See Clayborne Carson, ed., *The Papers of Martin Luther King Jr.: Rediscovering Precious Values* (Berkeley: University of California, 1994), 261.

Dr. King's friend Rabbi Abraham Joshua Heschel drew a similar lesson. (Dr. King was supposed to attend a Passover seder at Heschel's house but was killed two weeks before Passover.) Heschel delivered a speech in 1961 at the White House Conference on Religion and Race. He caught President Kennedy's attention when he opened with the words, "At the first conference on religion and race, the main participants were Pharaoh and Moses. Moses' words were: 'Thus says the Lord, the God of Israel, let My people go that they may celebrate a feast to Me.' While Pharaoh retorted: 'Who is the Lord, that I should heed this voice and let Israel go? I do not know the Lord, and moreover I will not let Israel go.' The outcome of that summit meeting has not come to an end."[7] With one sentence Heschel brought the Exodus story to bear upon a pressing issue. He also subtly gave it a new emphasis. In the Bible the story is not concerned primarily about the abolishment of slavery or racism as institutions. The Israelites continue the practice of slavery in Promised Land. Rather, the focus in the biblical text is the Israelites' freedom from Egypt so that they can serve God. Heschel shifts the focus to that of race relations. He shows the way the Bible's message can be reinterpreted and understood in new contexts. This openness to interpretation is what makes it relevant and sacred to every generation. That is not to say that we can interpret the Bible any way we wish. Rather, we trust knowledgeable teachers and precedents to shape our thinking. We recognize that while our situations change, human nature does not. God's message is still one we need to hear.

The Exodus message speaks in modern America not just to the message of race. It also speaks to the personal histories and values of Jews and Christians. In a recent class I asked members of my synagogue what the Exodus story meant to them. Did it affect

---

7. See Abraham Joshua Heschel, "On Race and Religion," in *The Insecurity of Freedom* (New York: Macmillan, 1963). Also available at http://voicesofde mocracy.umd.edu/heschel-religion-and-race-speech-text/.

their self-understanding? Could they see themselves in the story? All of them said yes. They frequently connected the Exodus with their family history. Many had grandparents and great-grandparents who immigrated to the United States from Europe. They fled poverty and persecution to build a better in life in America. They also saved future generations of their families, as most Jews who stayed in Europe were killed during the Holocaust. The members of my synagogue saw their grandparents' and great-grandparents' journey as a modern Exodus from oppression to freedom. America was their Promised Land. Europe was their Egypt. More recent Jewish immigrants echoed this message. Between 1967 and 1991, almost half of the entire Jewish population of the Soviet Union left it for freedom in Israel, America, and other Western countries. They saw their journey as an exodus from oppression to freedom.

In churches where I have led Passover seders, I've asked the same question. Some draw on their family history. More often, however, participants saw the Exodus in the context of their spiritual journeys. *A participant who became a Christian later in life saw crossing the Red Sea as a symbol for baptism. He had fled the oppression of his past life for freedom as a believer and follower of Jesus.* Others saw it as confirmation that God keeps his promises. God had promised the Israelites freedom and the Promised Land. After four hundred years of slavery, many had given up on that promise. Yet, through Moses God delivers the people. God will follow through on his promises, several participants said. Those promises include eternal life and a more peaceful world. Several other participants saw the Exodus in terms of their own struggles as members of a group and as individuals. Some women saw the Exodus story as a paradigm from gaining freedom from the past and strengthening their role in the church. Some saw the story as embodying the eternal struggle between tyranny and freedom, and they believed the story resonated strongly with American history and values.

One year I led a seder for those who struggled with addictions to alcohol and drugs. I shared a teaching from a nineteenth-century rabbi who universalized the meaning of Egypt. The Hebrew word for "Egypt," he noted, is *mitzrayim*. If we divide up *mitzrayim* into syllables, we get *mi-tzar-yim*. *Mi* means "from." *Tzar* can mean "narrowness," or a "narrow place." *Yim* makes the noun to which it is attached into a plural word. Thus, we can read the word *mitzrayim* as "from narrow places." These narrow places, said the nineteenth-century rabbi, are not geographic locales. They are narrow places in our mind and spirit. The message of the Exodus is that God can deliver us from those places. It is an early affirmation of what the Gospel of John would later proclaim, "The truth will set you free" (John 8:32).

The narrow places from which God can set us free include dependency on drugs or alcohol. Addiction is a form of enslavement. We lose control over our actions because our brains are subsumed by chemicals. God does not desire us to be oppressed in this way. The Exodus affirms that we can gain our freedom. These narrow places can also include an addiction to materialism, prejudice, a grudge, or an affair. We often become slaves to such pursuits through our own actions. We even know they are destroying us, yet we struggle to find a way out. Others may urge us to change, but we cannot find a way. We are like the pharaoh depicted in the Bible in Exodus 10:7. Pharaoh's advisors say to him, "'How long will this man trap us in a corner like this? Let the people go so they can worship the LORD their God. Don't you

Moses had become accustomed to his role as a shepherd and son-in-law of a local Midianite priest. At the burning bush, God reminded him of his ancestry and responsibility. Freedom takes courage, and courage is not easy. The Exodus story reiterates this message every year.

get it? Egypt is being destroyed!'" Our addictions or arrogance stand in the way of our freedom.

The message of the Exodus is God does not want us to remain in this state. Faith can set us free. The Exodus is a story for each of us. One of the biggest barriers to the Israelites attaining this faith while they were in Egypt was their complacency. They had accepted their situation. Even if slavery was oppressive, it was still predictable. Moses' role was to ignite the Israelites' passion for freedom. It was to wake them up out of the slumber of acceptance. God had performed the same act for Moses. Moses had become accustomed to his role as a shepherd and son-in-law of a local Midianite priest. At the burning bush, God reminded him of his ancestry and responsibility. Freedom takes courage, and courage is not easy. The Exodus story reiterates this message every year. The Israelites had to believe they could be free before they knew exactly how they would get there. They needed faith before they could find freedom. They needed to begin the journey before they had all the directions. So do we.

CHAPTER 10

CELEBRATING THE PASSOVER SEDER YOURSELF

A Haggadah for Home Use by Christians and Jews

A fter exploring the meaning of the Passover, are you ready to try it? Perhaps you have been asked to organize a Passover meal at your church. Or perhaps you are going to try it for the first time at home. This chapter will guide you through the process.

PREPARATION

It's best to start planning several months ahead of the actual seder date. If you are planning to hold the seder on the traditional first night of Passover, you need not worry about the date. You can look at an online calendar of Jewish holidays and know when the first night of Passover is for the next two thousand years! Several churches, however, will hold a seder on a different date. I recommend this practice because it allows you to invite Jewish guests (and to attend seder at a synagogue or friend's home) and avoids the suggestion that this Christian seder is replacing the traditional Jewish one. Some churches hold a seder on Maundy Thursday, consistent with the Christian tradition linking the Passover seder to the Last Supper. Others do it during the eight days of Passover, but not on the first night or second nights if they are inviting more traditional Jewish families, who will be hosting seders of their own on those evenings. Some even host a seder during the week before or after Passover, so as to avoid direct linkage with the Jewish observance of the holiday. From a planning perspective, the most important task is to choose the date and send out an invitation or save-the-date.

The next step is to plan for the meal. Most Christian and interfaith seders try to observe the traditional Jewish dietary laws of Passover. Thus, telling everyone who may cook or bring food to avoid any bread products is essential. You may want to guide potential hosts to these websites—www.urj.org and www.rabbimoffic.com—which outline the various dietary restrictions. One of the most confusing restrictions is on wine. There is kosher wine and kosher-for-Passover wine. The difference is the kosher-for-Passover wine must be made from a mold that has not been grown on bread (such as sugar or fruit) and must exclude several certain preservatives, like potassium sorbate. Most kosher wines are also kosher-for-Passover, but be sure to check for an official-looking "P" on the label.

One host should be responsible for acquiring all the necessary Passover items. These are described in chapters 5 and 6. They can generally be purchased all together through a Jewish goods store in person or online. Matzah is usually available at the supermarket, but it can also be special ordered.

With the food prepared and ritual items acquired, the host then prints copies of a Haggadah. The following is a Haggadah especially written for churches and families seeking to conduct an authentic Passover seder. You can also find other recommended hagaddahs at www.rabbimoffic.com.

A PASSOVER HAGGADAH

WELCOME
KADESH, SANCTIFICATION OF THE DAY

> *Note: it is not critical to have just one leader. The role of leader can change throughout the ceremony.*

Leader

Now in the presence of loved ones and friends,
With all the symbols of festive rejoicing before us,
we gather for our sacred celebration.
We gather to observe the Passover,
as it is written:

Group

"You shall keep the Feast of Unleavened Bread, for on this day I brought you out of Egypt. You shall observe this day for all time" (Exodus 12:17).[1]

This Haggadah incorporates the traditional readings and songs in Hebrew and English. The translations are my own. The retelling of the Passover story was drawn in large part from a text written by Rabbi Rachel Barenblat, which was used and edited with her permission.

1. For the Haggadah, I have used my own scriptural translations from the Hebrew for the Old Testament.

> *One may also wish to mention that Jesus and the disciples studied this story and observed this holiday the evening before his crucifixion. We come together to remember and relive that evening.*

LIGHTING THE FESTIVAL CANDLES

Leader

First we light the holiday candles, saying thank you, God, for bringing our family and friends together to celebrate Passover.

Group

May the festival lights we now kindle inspire us to use our powers
To heal and not harm,
To help and not hinder,
To serve You, O God of freedom.

> *In Jewish tradition the holiday candles symbolize peace in the home. They are traditionally lit by the matriarch of the family. To honor this tradition, you may wish to invite a senior female faith leader in the community or your family matriarch to the light the candles.*

Group

Blessed be the Lord, Our God, who has commanded us to kindle the holiday candles. Amen.

Baruch atah, Adonai, eloheinu melech ha'olam, asher kidshanu b'mitzvotav v'tzivanu l'hadlik ner shel Yom Tov.

בָּרוּךְ אַתָּה יְיָ אֱלֹהֵינוּ מֶלֶךְ הָעוֹלָם אֲשֶׁר קִדְּשָׁנוּ בְּמִצְוֹתָיו, וְצִוָּנוּ לְהַדְלִיק נֵר שֶׁל יוֹם טוֹב.

Leader

We also honor the holiness of this day by reciting the traditional Hebrew blessing of joy. It is said on the eve of all Jewish holidays and sacred occasions.

Group

Blessed are you, Adonai, sovereign of all worlds, who has kept us alive, sustained us, and enabled us to reach this time of joy.

Baruch atah, Adonai, eloheinu melech ha'olam, shecheyanu v'kiy'manu v'higiyanu lazman hazeh.

בָּרוּךְ אַתָּה יְיָ אֱלֹהֵינוּ מֶלֶךְ הָעוֹלָם, שֶׁהֶחֱיָנוּ וְקִיְּמָנוּ וְהִגִּיעָנוּ לַזְמַן הַזֶּה.

EXPLANATION OF THE PASSOVER SYMBOLS

Leader

The meal we will now share is one of the oldest continuous religious rituals in the Western world. It began on the eve of the Israelite Exodus from Egypt. We recall this historic event and honor the God who made it possible by telling and experiencing the Passover story. This ceremony is known as a *seder*.

In Hebrew, the word *seder* means "order." The ceremony proceeds in a precise order. We use each of these different items in a particular part of the ceremony. Let us look at the items on our seder plates and learn about what they mean.

Participant

What is the significance of the shank bone?

Leader

The shank bone, known in Hebrew as the *zeroah*, symbols the lamb offered as a sacrifice at the Temple in Jerusalem two thousand years ago. The lamb symbolizes God's mercy in redeeming the Israelites from slavery in Egypt. In Christian tradition, the lamb symbolizes Jesus, the Lamb of God, whose sacrifice frees believers from the sins of the world.

Participant

What is the significance of the matzah?

Leader
(hold up matzah)

The matzah is unleavened bread symbolizing the haste with which the Israelites had to leave Egypt. They had no time to let their bread rise. On most Jewish holidays, we bless two loaves of bread, symbolizing the additional sacrifice offered at the Jerusalem Temple on holidays. We follow that custom and also add a third piece of matzah to recognize the special obligation to remember the Exodus from Egypt. The three pieces of matzah also represent the three Jewish patriarchs: Abraham, Isaac, and Jacob. In Christian tradition, the three pieces of matzah can represent God's presence as the Father, Son, and Holy Ghost.

Participant

What is the significance of the egg?

Leader
(point to egg)

The egg, known in Hebrew as the *beitzah*, symbolizes the beginning of spring. It also is a reminder of the roasted egg offered at the Jerusalem Temple during Passover. In Christian tradition, the egg can represent Jesus' emergence from death into eternal life.

Participant

What is the significance of the *maror*?

Leader

The *maror*, or bitter herbs, reminds us of the bitterness of slavery.

Participant

What is the significance of the *charoset*?

Leader

The *charoset* is a mixture of chopped apples, cinnamon, nuts, and wine. It symbolizes the mortar used by the enslaved Israelites.

Participant

What is the significance of the parsley?

Leader

The parsley symbolizes the springtime and the rebirth of the Jewish people as they were redeemed from Egypt. We also dip it in salt water to remember of the tears of slavery.

EXPLANATION OF THE WINE (LEADER OR PARTICIPANT)

During this meal we will drink four cups of wine (or grape juice). These four cups represent the four times God promises in the Torah to redeem the Israelites from Egypt. "Therefore say to the children of Israel, 'I am the LORD. I will free you from the burdens of the Egyptians and deliver you from their bondage. I will redeem you with an outstretched arm and with mighty acts of chastisement. I will take you as my people and I will be your God'" (Exodus 6:6-7). The wine is usually red, recalling the blood the Israelites sprinkled on their doorposts so that their children would be "passed over" during the tenth plague of Egypt.

We turn now to the first cup of wine, known as the Cup of Holiness.

KOS KIDDUSH, THE FIRST CUP OF WINE

Leader

God promised our people freedom. With cups of wine, we recall each one of God's promises. The wine reminds us of the sweetness of life and the joy we feel when we are together.

We take up the Kiddush cup and proclaim the holiness of this Day of Deliverance!

Group

We praise You, O God, King of the Universe, Who created the Fruit of the Vine!

Baruch Atah Adonai Eloheinu Melech HaOlam Borei Pree-HaGafen.

בָּרוּךְ אַתָּה יְיָ אֱלֹהֵינוּ מֶלֶךְ הָעוֹלָם בּוֹרֵא פְּרִי הַגָּפֶן.

KARPAS—DIPPING OF GREENS IN SALT WATER

Leader

Salt water reminds us of the tears we cried when we were slaves, while green vegetables are symbols of the new life that grows in the spring.

Group

Praised are You, O Lord our God, King of the Universe, Who creates the Fruit of the Earth.

(Dip parsley in salt water and eat.)

YAHATZ, BREAKING THE MIDDLE MATZAH

Leader

Now I break the middle matzah and conceal one half as the *afikomon*. Later we will share it, as the Passover offering itself was shared in Jerusalem. We say together the ancient words that join us with our own people and with all who are hungry, remembering that our freedom is connected with the freedom of people everywhere.

Group

(Hold up Matzah)

This is the bread which our ancestors ate in Egypt. Let all who are hungry come and eat.

Let all who are needy come in and share the hope of Passover.

This year we celebrate here. Next year in the land of Israel.

Now we are still in slavery. Next year we may be free.

(Set matzah down without eating any.)

THE FOUR QUESTIONS

Leader

"We will go, young and old. We will go with our sons and our daughters . . . for we must observe the Lord's festival" (Exodus 10:9).

So it was said before the first Passover observance.

To this day, our children continue to join in our observance.

Child

Why is this night different from all other nights?

Children

On all other nights, we eat either leavened bread or *matzah*; on this night, why only *matzah*?

On all other nights, we eat all kinds of herbs; on this night, why do we especially eat bitter herbs?

On all other nights, we do not dip herbs at all; on this night why do we dip them twice?

On all other nights, we eat in an ordinary manner; why tonight do we dine with special ceremony?

Leader

These are all good questions. Why do we eat *matzah* on Passover?

Participant

Matzah recalls that the dough prepared by our people had no time to rise before the final act of Redemption. The raw dough they put on their backs baked into matzah.

Leader

Why do we eat bitter herbs at the seder?

Participant

To remind us of the bitter lives the slaves had while working for Pharaoh in Egypt.

Leader

Why do we dip foods twice at the seder?

Participant

The green vegetables remind us that spring is here and that new life grows around us.

The salt water reminds us of the tears of the slaves. We remember the happy and sad times together.

Group

Wherever slavery and oppression remain, we taste its bitterness.

Leader

Why do we dine with special ceremony?

Participant

To remind us that once we were slaves and now we are free! Eating with leisure and ceremony is a sign of our freedom.

Leader

We should feel as though we ourselves were rescued from Egypt, as it is written: "And you shall explain to your child on that day, it is because of what the Lord did for me when I, *myself*, went forth from Egypt."

Group

Still we remember: It was we who were slaves, we who were strangers. And therefore, we recall these words as well:

Leader

"You shall not oppress a stranger, for you know the feelings of the stranger" (Exodus 22:21).

Group

"For you were strangers in the land of Egypt" (Exodus 22:21).

FOUR KINDS OF CHILDREN

Leader

We all learn differently. The ancient Jewish sages honored those differences by imagining four different kinds of children who ask four different questions about Passover.

Participant

The wise child is eager to celebrate the holidays. She asks, "What is the meaning of the general rules and practices God commanded us concerning the Passover?" You shall tell her the Exodus story and teach her all the laws and practices of Passover.

Participant

The rebellious child does not participate with a full heart in the ceremony. He is still searching for answers. He asks, "What is the meaning of this ritual *to you*?" You shall tell him that Passover represents the freedom God gives *to us*. My freedom is tied to your freedom, and we are all part of one sacred community.

Participant

The simple child is innocent, naïve. He wants to understand the story of Passover. You shall tell him the basic outline of the Passover story and fill in the details as he grows.

Participant

There is also the child who does not know how to ask. She is shy and keeps to herself. You shall talk to her with patience and understanding, and open the way by saying to her: "We celebrate the Passover because of what God did for us when we came forth from Egypt."

THE STORY OF FREEDOM

THE EXODUS
A story in seven short chapters
1.

Once upon a time the Jewish people journeyed to the land of Egypt. They lived there in peace and prosperity, with Joseph rising to high position in Pharaoh's court. They were well respected and well regarded.

2.

Generations passed and they remained in Egypt. In time, a new pharaoh ascended to the throne. He found the Israelites threatening and different, and ordered them enslaved.

In fear of rebellion, Pharaoh decreed that all Hebrew newborn males be killed. Two midwives named Shifrah and Puah defied his orders, claiming that "the Hebrew women are so hardy, they give birth before we arrive!" Through their courage, a boy survived.

Fearing for his safety, his family placed him in a basket and he floated down the Nile. He was found, and adopted, by Pharaoh's daughter, who named him Moshe because *min ha-mayim m'shitihu*, from the water she drew him forth. She hired his mother, Yocheved, as his wet nurse. Thus he survived to adulthood and was raised as a prince of Egypt.

3.

Although a child of privilege, as he grew he became aware of the slaves who worked in the brickyards of his father. When he saw an overseer mistreat a slave, he struck the overseer and killed him. Fearing retribution, he set out across the Sinai alone.

God spoke to him from a burning bush, which though it flamed was not consumed. The Voice called him to lead the Hebrew people to freedom. Moses argued with God, pleading inadequacy, but God disagreed. Sometimes our responsibilities choose us.

4.

Moses returned to Egypt with his brother Aaron and went to Pharaoh to argue the injustice of slavery. He gave Pharaoh a mandate which resounds through history: "Let my people go!"

Pharaoh refused, and Moses warned him that Mighty God would strike the Egyptian people. These threats were not idle: ten terrible plagues were unleashed upon the Egyptians. Only when his nation lay in ruins did Pharaoh agree to let the Israelites go.

5.

Fearful that Pharaoh would change his mind, the Israelites fled, not waiting for their bread dough to rise. (For this reason we eat unleavened bread as we take part in their journey.) Our people did not leave Egypt alone; a "mixed multitude" went with them. From this we learn that liberation is not for us alone, but for all the nations of the earth.

6.

Pharaoh's army followed the Israelites to the Red Sea. While the sea parted for the Israelites, it closed in on Pharaoh's troops. We mourn, even now, that some of the innocents in Pharaoh's army drowned.

7.

To this day we relive and remember our freedom, that we may not become complacent, that we may always rejoice and never take that freedom for granted.

DAYENU

"*Dayenu*" is a song of gratitude, of thanksgiving. We acknowledge *several* major biblical events and proclaim after each of them: "It would have been enough!"[2]

	(A singable English version:)
Ilu ho-tsi, ho-tsi-a-nu,	Had He brought all, brought all of us,
Ho-tsi-a-nu mi-Mitz-ra-yim,	brought all of us out from Egypt,
Ho-tsi-a-nu mi-Mitz-ra-yim,	brought all of us out from Egypt,
Da-ye-nu!	then it would have been enough!

---

2. Links to audio files and music can be found in the Resources section at http://www.rabbimoffic.com/category/resource-center/.

CHORUS:

Dai, da-ye-nu,

Dai, da-ye-nu,

Dai, da-ye-nu,

Da-ye-nu, da-ye-nu, da-ye-nu!

Dai, da-ye-nu,

Dai, da-ye-nu,

Dai, da-ye-nu,

Da-ye-nu, da-ye-nu!

Ilu na-tan, na-tan la-nu,

Na-tan la-nu et-ha-Sha-bat,

Na-tan la-nu et-ha-Sha-bat,

Da-ye-nu!

(CHORUS)

Ilu na-tan, na-tan la-nu,

Na-tan la-nu et-ha-To-rah,

Na-tan la-nu et-ha-To-rah,

Da-ye-nu!

(CHORUS)

CHORUS:

Dai, da-ye-nu,

Dai, da-ye-nu,

Dai, da-ye-nu,

Da-ye-nu, da-ye-nu, da-ye-nu!

Dai, da-ye-nu,

Dai, da-ye-nu,

Dai, da-ye-nu,

Da-ye-nu, da-ye-nu!

Had He given, given to us,

given to us all the Sabbath,

given to us all the Sabbath,

then it would have been enough!

(CHORUS)

Had He given, given to us,

given to us all the Torah,

given to us all the Torah,

then it would have been enough!

(CHORUS)

RECOLLECTION OF THE TEN PLAGUES

Leader

The Jewish sages taught that, while watching the Egyptians succumb to the ten plagues, the angels broke into songs of jubilation. God rebuked them, saying "My creatures are perishing, and you sing praises?"

Group

As we recite each plague, we spill a drop of wine—symbol of joy—from our cups. Our joy in our liberation will always be tarnished by the pain visited upon the Egyptians.

Dam (Blood)
Tzfarde'ah (Frogs)
Kinim (Lice)
Arov (Insect swarms)
Dever (Cattle plague)
Sh'chin (Boils)
Barad (Hail)
Arbeh (Locusts)
Choshech (Darkness)
Makat B'chorot (Death of the Firstborn)

Leader

These plagues are in the past, but today's world holds plagues as well. Let us spill drops of wine as we recite: these ten modern plagues.

Apathy in the face of evil
Brutal torture of the helpless
Cruel mockery of the old and the weak
Despair of human goodness
Envy of the joy of others
Falsehood and deception corroding our faith
Greed
Hatred of learning and culture
Instigation of war and aggression
Justice delayed, justice denied[3]

---

3. Rabbi Rachel Barenblat, http://velveteenrabbi.com/.

THE THREE SYMBOLS

Leader

Rabban Gamliel, the teacher of Saul of Tarsus who became the Apostle Paul, taught that each of us must study in depth the meaning of the matzah, the *maror,* and *zeroah.* We have already touched on the basics of what they mean. Let us explore further.

Participant

Matzah is the bread of simplicity. It is flour and water. It reminds us that we do not need the fancy and the elaborate to sustain us. We depend only on God. Matzah also represents the fragility of freedom. The Israelites knew Pharaoh would soon renege on his promises. Tyranny dies hard. They had to seize the moment and run for their freedom. We thank God they did. And matzah represents affliction. Our ancestors had little to sustain them. So do many in our world today. We share the matzah with them in hopes they may find sustenance and nourishment in our world abounding with blessings.

> *Some Christians interpret the perforations on the matzah as symbolic of the piercings of Jesus on the cross. Jesus is the Bread of Life, afflicted in sacrifice yet nourishing the world.*

Participant

Maror is the bitter herb of slavery. Even if we enjoy the blessings of freedom, we share the pain of those who suffer still. We relive the pain of the Israelites so as to propel us into bringing the blessings of freedom to our world. Bitterness does not last forever. The taste burns, but it recedes. With our commitment, so does the pain of suffering. So does the hurt of injustice. As Theodore Parker said, the moral arc of the universe is long, yet it bends toward justice.

Participant

The shank bone represents the ancient sacrifice of the paschal lamb. For Jews it also symbolizes the Temple that stood in Jerusalem. The Temple was God's home on earth. It was there that the priests sang the psalms of Israel. It was there where the people gathered for the holidays and moved closer to God through song, prayer, and sacrifice. When it was destroyed by the Romans, Judaism could have died. Yet, God's presence covers the world. The Temple remains in our hearts. This shank bone connects us to a glorious past even as we build an extraordinary future.

For Christians, as we noted earlier, the shank bone can be seen as symbolizing Jesus as the sacrificial lamb of God. The significance of this designation is described by John the Baptist, "Look! The Lamb of God who takes away the sin of the world. This is the one about whom I said, 'He who comes after me is really greater than me because he existed before me.' Even I didn't recognize him, but I came baptizing with water so that he might be made known to Israel" (John 1:29-31).

EATING THE MATZAH AND *MAROR*

Leader

The time has come to eat the matzah and *maror*. First we say a blessing.

Group

Blessed are you, Eternal God, Sovereign of the Universe, who brings forth bread from the earth.

Baruch Atah Adonai Eloheinu Melech HaOlam hamotzei lechem min haaretz.

בָּרוּךְ אַתָּה יְיָ אֱלֹהֵינוּ מֶלֶךְ הָעוֹלָם, הַמּוֹצִיא לֶחֶם מִן הָאָרֶץ.

(We eat a piece of matzah)

> We can also recall the words the Apostle Paul delivered to the church in Corinth in which he compares the process of making matzah with finding simplicity and truth. "Don't you know that a little yeast works through the whole batch of dough? Get rid of the old yeast that you may be a new batch without yeast—as you really are. For Christ, our Passover Lamb, has been sacrificed. Therefore let us keep the festival, not with the old yeast, the yeast of malice and wickedness, but with bread made without yeast, the bread of sincerity and truth" (1 Corinthians 5:5-8).

Leader and Group

We taste now the bitterness of slavery. "We praise You, O Lord our God, King of the Universe, who commands us to eat of the bitter herbs."

Leader

A great first-century Jewish leader named Hillel lived while the Jerusalem Temple still stood. He used to make a sandwich with matzah and *maror*, following the biblical commandment, "They shall eat the Passover offering together with matzah and *maror*" (Numbers 9:11).

Group

We follow that practice today and make a Hillel sandwich.

(The bottom matzah is broken, and each participant takes two pieces with some bitter herbs in between forming a sandwich. All then eat the "Hillel Sandwich.")

THE SECOND CUP OF WINE

Leader

The second cup of wine is known as the cup of redemption. We remember God's promise to redeem the Israelites from Egypt, just as God redeems us today.

Group

We praise You, O God, King of the Universe, Creator of the Fruit of the Vine!

Baruch Atah Adonei Elohanu Melech Haolam Borei Pri Hagafen.

בָּרוּךְ אַתָּה יְיָ אֱלֹהֵינוּ מֶלֶךְ הָעוֹלָם בּוֹרֵא פְּרִי הַגָּפֶן

(All drink the second cup of wine.)

RACHATZ (WASHING)

Leader

The Passover meal always includes a traditional hand washing. The goal is not just hygiene. It is purity before God. (A pitcher may be brought to the table along with a towel. Some communities may choose to have only the leader wash his or her hands as a symbolic act for the entire community.)

Christians may also use this time to consider and recall the moment during the Last Supper where Jesus rose and washed the feet of his disciples.

SHULHAN ORECH, THE FESTIVE MEAL IS SERVED

TZAFUN, THE SEARCH FOR THE HIDDEN MATZAH

Leader

The children now search for the *afikomon*. We find and eat it to remember the offering of the Passover lamb, which was eaten at the end of the meal. By eating this matzah last, we also let the taste of freedom linger in our mouths.

(When it is found, the leader distributes pieces of it to each child.)

GRACE AFTER THE MEAL

Leader

Jewish tradition instructs us to say a longer prayer of gratitude *after* the meal than before it. Now that we are satisfied, we may forget the grace with which God has blessed us. Thus, we express our gratitude for it.

Group

Let us praise the Eternal, of Whose bounty we have partaken and by Whose goodness we live.

On this Festival of Matzot, inspire us to goodness. On this Festival of Freedom, make us a blessing. On this Festival of Pesach, preserve us in life.

All-Merciful, You are our Source.

Sustain us with honorable work.

Make us worthy of the promise of a world that is yet to come.

May the One who blessed Abraham, Isaac, and Jacob, Sarah, Rebecca, Rachel, and Leah,

bless this home, this table, and all assembled here; and may all our loved ones share our blessing.

May the One who brings harmony into the spheres on high bring peace to earth for all humanity.

Kos B'raha—The Third Cup, the Cup of Blessing

Leader

Together we take the third cup of wine, recalling the divine promise to bless the people Israel.

Group

We praise You, O Lord our God, King of the universe, Who created the Fruit of the Vine.

Baruch Atah Adonai Eloheinu Melech HaOlam Borei Pri HaGafen.

בָּרוּךְ אַתָּה יְיָ אֱלֹהֵינוּ מֶלֶךְ הָעוֹלָם בּוֹרֵא פְּרִי הַגָּפֶן

Kos Eliyahu, the Cup of Elijah

Leader

The prophet Elijah heralds the coming of a new day. He symbolizes the reconciliation of families, of communities, of nations, of the world. We sing a song welcoming him to our Passover table, praying for his presence to illuminate our world.

> *Leader can also discuss here the connection between Elijah the prophet and John the Baptist. The biblical Book of Malachi ends with God telling the people that Elijah will come before the "awesome, fearful day of the Lord." Elijah's role is to announce the coming of the Messiah. John the Baptist serves that role in the New Testament.*

Group

ELIYAHU HANAVI	ELIJAH THE PROPHET[4]
Eliyahu hanavi	Elijah the prophet
Eliyahu hatishbi,	Elijah the returning,
Eliyahu hagil'adi—	Elijah the Giladi—
Bim'hera yavoh eleinu,	May he soon come to us,
im mashiach ben David. (x2)	with the messiah son of David. (x2)

THE FOURTH CUP

Leader

The fourth cup of wine represents God's fourth declaration of redemption: "I will claim you for me as a people, and I will be your God" (Exodus 7). For this final cup, let our coming together in celebration bless the sweetness of the fruit of the vine.

Group

Blessed are you, Adonai our God, Ruler of the universe, Creator of the Fruit of the Vine.

Baruch atah, Adonai, eloheinu melech ha'olam, borei pri hagafen.

בָּרוּךְ אַתָּה יְיָ אֱלֹהֵינוּ מֶלֶךְ הָעוֹלָם בּוֹרֵא פְּרִי הַגָּפֶן

CONCLUSION

Leader

The seder service now concludes:

---

4. Links to audio files and music can be found in the Resources section at http://www.rabbimoffic.com/category/resource-center/.

Its rites observed in full,
Its purpose revealed.

Group

This privilege we share will ever be renewed.
Until God's plan is known in full,
God's highest blessing sealed.

Leader

Peace!

Group

Peace for us! For everyone!

Leader

This is our hope. May we see Jerusalem in its glory, the city of peace sending its light to all the world.

Group
(Repeat three times—Increase tempo every two verses)

Le-Shanah Haba'ah B'Ye-ru-sha-la-yim	Next year in Jerusalem!
Le-Shanah Haba'ah B'Ye-ru-sha-la-yim	Next year in Jerusalem!
Le-Shanah Haba'ah B'Ye-ru-sha-la-yim	Next year in Jerusalem!
Le-Shanah Haba'ah B'Ye-ru-sha-la-yim	Next year in Jerusalem!
Next year, may all be free!	Next year, may all be free!
Let us sing![5]	Let us sing!

5. Links to audio files and music can be found in the Resources section at http://www.rabbimoffic.com/category/resource-center/.

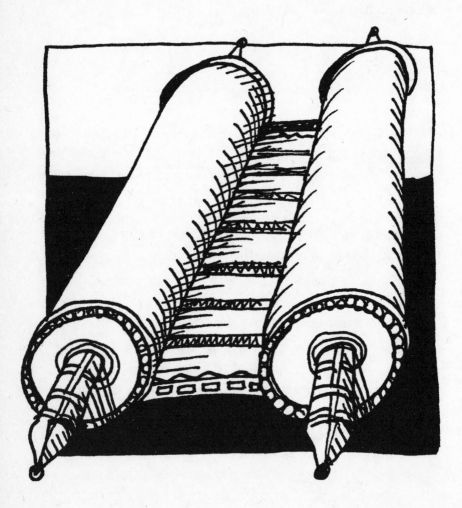

EPILOGUE

Your Letter in the Scroll

The Exodus story was first recorded on ancient parchment known as a Torah scroll. Jewish legend says the first Torah scroll was written by Moses atop Mount Sinai. The oldest one we have today was discovered among the Dead Sea scrolls and dates from the second century BCE. The words in a Torah scroll are written with a quill, usually from a turkey feather, using a special ink mixture. Torah scrolls have been written in the same way for the last two thousand years. Every letter is precisely etched by pious scribes who have dedicated their lives to this vocation. If they make a mistake writing the name of God, they start the entire page over. Every letter is sacred, and a scroll with a missing letter is invalid and incomplete.

In the Exodus story, each of us is like a letter in the scroll. The story is incomplete without us. We enter the story with different experiences, hopes, and visions of the Promised Land. But we know we cannot get there alone. We need the other letters.

Having read this book, you have added your letter to the scroll. From now on the story will be incomplete without you. May it bring you strength as you journey from slavery to freedom, from despair to hope, from yesterday to tomorrow. Amen.

WHAT EVERY CHRISTIAN
NEEDS TO KNOW ABOUT PASSOVER

A Study Guide
for Individuals and Groups

This study guide examines parts of each chapter for further spiritual and personal exploration.

1. FROM SLAVERY TO FREEDOM: THE BIBLICAL EXODUS

Moses noticed the burning bush
Early Christian commentators drew a connection between God in the burning bush, and Mary the mother of God. As Old Testament scholar Ellen F. Davis has put it, "Mary, who carried God in her belly and later in her arms, yet did not dissolve to ash—she is herself the bush that burns perpetually, yet is not consumed."[1] In this way, the burning bush might become an Advent image, or a Christmas image. Does this image resonate with you? What do you think of the idea that Mary is like the burning bush?

---

1. Ellen F. Davis, *Getting Involved With God: Rediscovering the Old Testament* (Lanham, MD: Cowley, 2001), 46.

The Hebrew word Moses used in answering God's voice highlights his readiness to act. Moses says "Hineni, I'm here" (Exodus 3:4).

When have you heard God calling you? When have you responded "I am here"? Have you ever heard God calling and turned aside, unwilling to say "I am here"?

2. Rituals of Freedom: The Celebration of Passover During the Lifetime of Jesus

It is Passover that Mary, Joseph, and the young Jesus are celebrating in Jerusalem in the second chapter of the Gospel of Luke.

Luke tells the story this way:

Each year his parents went to Jerusalem for the Passover Festival. When he was 12 years old, they went up to Jerusalem according to their custom. After the festival was over, they were returning home, but the boy Jesus stayed behind in Jerusalem. His parents didn't know it. Supposing that he was among their band of travelers, they journeyed on for a full day while looking for him among their family and friends. When they didn't find Jesus, they returned to Jerusalem to look for him. After three days they found him in the temple. He was sitting among the teachers, listening to them and putting questions to them. Everyone who heard him was amazed by his understanding and his answers. When his parents saw him, they were shocked. His mother said, "Child, why have you treated us like this? Listen! Your father and I have been worried. We've been looking for you!"

> Jesus replied, "Why were you looking for me? Didn't you
> know that it was necessary for me to be in my Father's house?"
> But they didn't understand what he said to them. (2:41-50)

Do you think there is special significance to the fact that this story happened during Passover, and not at another time of year?

Memory was ritualized.

One of the ways in which the church ritualizes memory is in the Lord's Supper: at the Lord's Supper, Christians remember Jesus' Last Supper.

How might it change your experience of the Lord's Supper to remember that at his Last Supper, Jesus was remembering God's liberating the Jewish people from bondage in Egypt?

Are there other ways your church community ritualizes memory?

Matzah also has something to teach us about freedom.

Different Christian communities use different kinds of bread in Holy Communion: some use wafers, some use fresh-baked loaves, some even use matzah.

What does Communion bread have to teach us about freedom?

Each of us can encounter God in simple places.

Where are the simple places you have encountered God?

3. AROUND THE TABLE: WHY PASSOVER IS A HOLIDAY CELEBRATED PRIMARILY AT HOME

"Table Fellowship"

When have you experienced table fellowship in your church? Can you remember a Eucharist that felt truly like a meal? When has the Eucharist felt more like true table fellowship, and when less so?

Have you experienced table fellowship at a potluck dinner—in the church social hall or at your home? At a church picnic? Does church "coffee hour" feel like real table fellowship? If not, how could the "table fellowship" aspects of that experience be deepened? What aspects of eating at a restaurant foster table fellowship, and what aspects of dining at restaurants feel at odds with table fellowship?

How do we treat most meals? Are they occasions for holiness?
What meals have you eaten in the last year that felt like occasions for holiness? What made them so? Would you like to infuse your day-to-day meals with a greater sense of holiness? What would help? Maybe praying before the meal? Maybe planting a vegetable garden, and increasing your own direct connection to the food on your table? Maybe eating more slowly? Maybe lighting candles?

We remember what happened to our ancestors. We derive meaning and direction from those memories.
What stories of things that happened to your ancestors do you derive meaning and direction from?

In my own spiritual journey, a formative moment happened around a Passover table.
What formative moments in your spiritual journey have happened around the table?

4. CLEANSE YOUR SPIRIT AND CLEANSE YOUR KITCHEN: HOW TO PREPARE FOR A PASSOVER SEDER

Lent is preparation for the celebration of remembering the crucifixion on Good Friday and the resurrection of Jesus on Easter Sunday

Do you observe Lent—perhaps by "giving up" or "taking on" something in the weeks before Good Friday and Easter? How has it helped you prepare for remembering Jesus' death on Good Friday and celebrating his resurrection on Easter Sunday? What similarities do you see between preparing for Passover and observing Lent?

Many make every effort to eliminate chametz *from their homes.*

How does the importance of ridding *chametz* from the Jewish home before Passover—and the detailed process for searching out every scrap of *chametz*—help you interpret Paul's words to the Corinthians "Clean out the old yeast so you can be a new batch of dough, given that you're supposed to be unleavened bread. Christ our Passover lamb has been sacrificed, so let's celebrate the feast with the unleavened bread of honesty and truth, not with old yeast or with the yeast of evil and wickedness" (1 Corinthians 5:7-8)?

Cleaning the home for Passover became the perfect means for cleaning the home for spring.

Some Jewish women have noted that the intense work of cleaning the house for Passover typically falls on women, and that there is, at best, an irony of having to do so much work to prepare for a festival of freedom. As Marge Piercy has put it "for many Jewish women, the housework around Pesach is burdensome and gives them all the spiritual zing of doing the laundry on a heavy day three times over."[2] Or, as Judy Sirota Rosenthal has written "It's so much work!" remains the refrain around women's preparation for Passover. The rigorous work of cleaning, shopping, and cooking are tasks we rarely consider in their own right. Most often, we think about them in terms of the goal and reward of the seder, not as rituals. But preparing for

---

2. Marge Piercy, *Pesach for the Rest of Us: Making the Passover Seder Your Own* (New York: Schocken Books, 2007), 20.

Passover could be very different if approached from a new perspective: Pesach is one of the three pilgrimage holidays, and the preparations for a pilgrimage enrich the process. People going on a serious climb or trek prepare by walking around their neighborhoods with heavy backpacks. We clean, search, and labor in our homes. Might this also constitute an important ritual preparation for our journey towards freedom?[3] How do you think you would experience all the prep work of Passover?

Read the story of Mary and Martha (Luke 10:38-42). How is the meaning of the story illuminated by Piercy's and Rosenthal's observations about Passover?

5. THE SEDER PLATE:
HOW RITUAL OBJECTS CONNECT US
TO ONE ANOTHER AND TO GOD

They may keep it on a special shelf in the china cupboard. They use it only once a year, yet it is hugely important—far more important than any other plate in the house.

Do you have special holiday dishes that you only use a few times a year? What meaning do they add to the meals when you use them? What would be lost from those meals if the special dishes vanished?

The seder plate is to Passover dinner what the chalice and paten are to the celebration of Communion.

---

3. Judy Sirota Rosenthal, "Preparing for the Pilgrimage," in Sharon Cohen Anisfeld, Tara Mohr, and Catherine Spector, eds., *The Women's Seder Sourcebook: Rituals and Readings for Use at the Passover Seder* (Woodstock: Jewish Lights, 2003), 11.

What kinds of plates and cups, patens and chalices, does your church use for Communion? Are they silver? Ceramic? Metal? Do you have certain feelings or associations when you sip Communion wine or juice from a silver cup, and different feelings or associations with a pottery cup? Do you experience Communion differently when you receive from one common cup, on the one hand, and when you are handed a small individual cup of wine or juice on the other hand?

The breaking of the middle Matzah

How might the breaking of the middle Matzah at Passover inform or enrich your understanding of Jesus' encounter with bread at the Last Supper? "After taking the bread and giving thanks, he broke it and gave it to them, saying, 'This is my body, which is given for you. Do this in remembrance of me'" (Luke 22:19).

According to the foremost rabbinical sage of the first century, Akiba, the Song of Songs is an allegory depicting the love between God and the people of Israel. It is, in effect, a sacred love poem. While this allegorizing may seem strange or surprising to some, it fits with a metaphor used throughout the Old Testament. The metaphor is that of marriage.

Many Christian interpreters have read the Song of Songs in a way similar to Rabbi Akiba—they have seen the Song as an allegory between God and the church. Does it make sense to you to read it as an allegory, or as the frankly erotic love poem it seems to me—or both?

The fifth symbol is the bitter herb, known in Hebrew as the *maror*. *It symbolizes the bitterness of slavery.*

Perhaps when Christians at a seder eat *maror*, they should remember not just painful things done to them. Perhaps they should also remember the bitter pain that the church has sometimes caused non-Christians, or the bitter pain that some Christian communities have caused other Christian communities. Can you think of a moment in church history when the church has been the agent of bitter pain? How might we recall that moment today and repent of it?

symbolizes the best way to respond to tragedy and suffering

Christian theologian Monika Hellwig has written that

> the reason for the Eucharistic celebration . . . is that by participating in the experience of the death of Jesus they may read in that death the unfinished agenda of the redemption of the world. It is from [this] Christian perspective . . . that a contemporary Roman Catholic theologian, J. B. Metz, is able to make the claim that the whole sense of celebrating Eucharist in the Christian community is that the future may appear "in the memory of suffering," in other words, that we may learn to write history upside down from the point of view of the loser or the vanquished, because it is there that the unfinished agenda appears.[4]

How do you practice this upside-down perspective in your own life? How is Hellwig's idea consistent with the themes of Passover? Might Jesus, who observed Passover every year of his life, have intended this when he instituted Holy Communion at the Last Supper?

another understanding of the egg

Eggs also feature, of course, in Easter celebrations. When next setting out eggs for a children's Easter egg hunt, you might ponder some of the meanings eggs have in Judaism. Did you know that Easter eggs are symbols of the Resurrection? Baby chickens break

---

4. Monika K. Hellwig, "The Christian Eucharist in Relation to Jewish Worship," *Journal of Ecumenical Studies*, 13 no 2 (Spring 1976): 136 [326].

forth from the egg in order to have new life, just as the living Jesus breaks out of the grave.

Symbols matter in religious life
What symbols matter most in your religious life?

6. BLESSING AND QUESTIONING: THE SEDER BEGINS

In a religious realm, ritual takes on even greater importance. It brings order to the universe. It brings transcendent meaning to the acts we perform.
What are the central rituals of your religious life? What important work do those rituals do? How do they bring transcendence into your life?

A blessing infuses a sacred dimension into what we experience.
What is a blessing?
In Judaism, all blessings begin with the words "Blessed are You, Lord Our God, King of the Universe" and they conclude with something specific to the thing occasioning the blessing "King of the Universe, who brings forth bread from the earth" (to be said before eating bread) or "creates the Fruit of the Vine" (to be said before drinking wine) or even "King of the Universe who varies the forms of His many creatures" (to be said when seeing something strange). Some Jews have the practice of trying to say one hundred blessings a day. How might it change your spiritual life to say more blessings? Can you imagine, tomorrow, proclaiming a blessing in response to three or five or seven things you encounter during your day?

In an important 1968 book on the Eucharist, Louis Bouyer said that these Jewish blessings proclaim three things—that there is a personal relationship between God and God's people; that God's blessing of God's people is central to the covenant or relationship between them; and that the blessing (over bread, wine, strangeness, and so forth) is the way that Jewish people respond to God. According to Bouyer, this three-part proclamation made its way from Judaism into Christians' Eucharistic prayers.[5] Do you see any or all aspects of this three-part proclamation in your own life of prayer and worship?

This is the bread of affliction that our fathers ate in the land of Egypt. Let all who are hungry, come and eat. Let all who are needy, come and celebrate Passover.
The New Testament, like the Passover Haggadah, is full of reminders and injunctions to feed the hungry. For example, the Epistle of James says

> My brothers and sisters, what good is it if people say they have faith but do nothing to show it? Claiming to have faith can't save anyone, can it? Imagine a brother or sister who is naked and never has enough food to eat. What if one of you said, "Go in peace! Stay warm! Have a nice meal!"? What good is it if you don't actually give them what their body needs? In the same way, faith is dead when it doesn't result in faithful activity. (James 2:14-17)

When, in your life, are you closest to the God who wants you to feed the hungry? When are you furthest away from that God?

---

5. As noted in Sean Edward Kinsella, "The Transformation of the Jewish Passover in an Early Christian Liturgy: The influence of the Passover *Haggadah* in the Apostolic Tradition," *Science et Esprit*, 52/2 (2000): 220.

7. "As Though You Yourself Journeyed from Slavery to Freedom": Telling the Passover Story

During the seder we are meant not so much to listen to the story, as we are meant to experience it. The text of the story frequently uses the first-person plural. Pharaoh enslaved us. God freed us.

What stories do people in your church community retell?

The kind of memory one practices during the seder—in which the twenty-first-century participants at the seder not only recall ancient enslavement and liberation, but recall enslavement and liberation as though it had happened to them—is called *anamnesis. Anamnesis* is the technical theological term for remembering something as though you had experienced it, and allowing the past to bear on your present. Jews are invited to practice anamnesis at the seder; Christians are invited to practice anamnesis at Communion—not just to recall Jesus' Last Supper as a dim historical memory, but to allow that past story to bear on the present in a unique and significant way, as though it were happening even now. What might it mean for your spiritual life to practice anamnesis—to allow the past of Jesus' Last Supper to infuse your present?

Dip your finger into your cup of wine and spatter out a drop for each plague. The drops of wine we spill symbolize the tears of the Egyptians.

As we are learning, wine plays an important role in the seder. How might the role of wine at the seder shape how you think about Jesus identifying himself as the true vine (John 15:1), and naming the cup of wine at the Last Supper as "the new covenant by my blood, which is poured out for you" (Luke 22:20)?

"Israel saw the amazing power of the Lord *against the Egyptians. The people were in awe of the* Lord, *and they believed in the* Lord *and in his servant Moses" (Exodus 14:31).*

A lot of churches read this passage from Exodus (14:10-31) on Easter (or on the Saturday night before Easter). Why? What does it have to do with Easter? What do you think of minister John Holbert's suggestion:

> God, it seems, on Easter Day and on every other day is finally the God of life, fully opposed to the powerful and ever-present forces of death. The story of Jesus' resurrection is hardly the first story of such an event in history. . . . There were the Hebrews, who built their very lives on the certain conviction that their God, YHWH, had, because of unbreakable love for them as a people, led them out of the horrors of Egyptian slavery, through the forbidding Sinai wilderness, into and out of the terrible Sea of Reeds, and at last into the land of promise. They proclaimed in story and song that on the west bank of that sea they were the hopeless captives of the cruel pharaohs, while on the east bank of the sea they were the people of YHWH. This is precisely the resurrection story of Israel.[6]

Many families also use this part of the seder to mention modern experiences of unjust suffering.

What experiences of modern unjust suffering feel most significant to you? If you were to symbolize those experiences with a food, what food would you pick, and why?

It reminds me to try to live the Passover message in my life.

What is the Passover message? How might you more fully live the Passover message in your life?

---

6. John C. Holbert, "Resurrection by Another Name," www.patheos.com /Progressive-Christian/Resurrection-Another-Name-John-Holbert-04-11-2014.

8. Praising and Singing: The Seder Concludes

Having Passover at home also makes it an opportunity for hospitality.

Perhaps one way to infuse our meals—during the Passover/Easter season, and all year long—with sacred meaning would be to extend greater hospitality. In Matthew 25, Jesus tells his friends and followers that every time they welcome a stranger or feed a hungry person, they are welcoming or feeding him, and every time they turn away a hungry person or a stranger, they are turning him away. This seems to be a message very consistent with the deep messages of Passover—the bread of affliction, welcoming the stranger, extending God's freedom to all. How might you open your table to a stranger or a hungry person? How do you react to the idea that when you make that gesture of welcome, you are not doing just a good deed— you are actually welcoming Jesus?

The Bible specifically commands saying grace after the meal.

Many Christians pray before meals, but few say a specific grace after a meal. What might the spiritual fruits of post-prandial praying be? If you were to write a prayer to say after lunch or dinner, what would your prayer say?

The singing of several songs unique to Passover.

Does singing play a significant role in your observance of Good Friday? Easter? What songs are significant to you? Why?

We learn from our experience there to welcome and love the stranger.

The Passover story has a lot to say about how we might think about and welcome strangers. The Christian story does too. Jesus, Mary, and Joseph, for example, became strangers themselves when they fled to Egypt in order to protect the baby Jesus' life. Does the Passover story, and the experience of Jesus fleeing to an alien country for safety, have any bearing on how you interact with or think about immigrants in your community?

9. FROM ANCIENT ISRAEL TO CONTEMPORARY AMERICA: THE UNIVERSAL STORY OF FREEDOM

I asked members of my synagogue what the Exodus story meant to them. Did it affect their self-understanding? Could they see themselves in the story?

What does the Exodus story mean to you? How does it affect your self-understanding? Where in the story do you see yourself?

ACKNOWLEDGMENTS

This book began in a series of classes I taught at the Fourth Presbyterian Church of Chicago. Those classes led to Passover seders with Fourth Presbyterian, Chicago Sinai Congregation, Holy Name Cathedral, and the Moody Bible Institute. I am grateful to all the students and participants in those seders. Your insights and questions shaped every page of this book.

I am also grateful for the members and leadership of the two extraordinary congregations I have served as rabbi: Chicago Sinai Congregation and Congregation Solel. Believing that Jewish wisdom and tradition needs to speak to the larger community, they gave me the encouragement and time to write and speak. Few rabbis are as blessed with such wise, accomplished, and generous lay leaders.

My agent, Steve Laube, helped me hone my message and found the perfect publisher in Abingdon Press. At Abingdon, I was guided by the experienced hands of Lil Copan, Pamela Clements, Cat Hoort, Brenda Smotherman, and Julie Gwinn. My editor, Lauren Winner, is simply extraordinary. An accomplished author and speaker whom I have long admired, she helped bring my life experience and voice into the text, turning what felt at first like an academic tome into a focused spiritual journey through the depths of Passover. I now refer to Lauren as my "editor for life."

Along the way I also benefitted from conversations with many pastors, priests, and rabbis, including Lillian Daniel, David Wood, John Cusick, Tom Hurley, John Vest, Christine Chakoian, Rich Darr, and many more. Several writing friends—especially Michael Hyatt,

Michele Cushatt, Dan Blank, and Jeff Goins—encouraged and inspired me throughout the creation of this book.

My patient family—Ari, Hannah, and Tam—give me endless love and grace. So do my parents, sister, and in-laws. Writers can be groggy, intense, and self-absorbed. Somehow they put up with me and are the greatest blessing of all.